MW01144550

1

STUDENT BOOK

Writing
for the Real World

AN INTRODUCTION TO GENERAL WRITING

Roger Barnard | Dorothy E Zemach

OXFORD
UNIVERSITY PRESS

Contents

1 Thinking about writing

IN THIS UNIT, YOU WILL ...

▶ think about different types of writing in everyday life

▶ think about the types of writing you do now in your own language and in English

▶ think about the types of English writing you will do in the future

▶ write a short email to your teacher

1 An email to a teacher

1 Read this email from a student to his teacher.

To:	Jennifer Kovacs
Cc:	
Subject:	Writing and me

Arial · 10 · B I U 田 · ⋮≡ ⋮≡ ⋮≡ | ≡ ≡ ≡ |

Dear Ms. Kovacs,

I would like to tell you about writing and me.

I really like writing in my own language. I often write papers for my classes and send emails to my friends.

At present, I don't write very much in English.

In the future, I want to write personal emails in English and I might write business letters and emails.

I'm looking forward to the writing class.

Sincerely,

Carlos Puentes

2 Are these statements true (T) or false (F)? Check (✓) the correct box.

		T	F
a	Jennifer Kovacs wrote the email.	☐	☐
b	Carlos likes writing in his own language.	☐	☐
c	He often writes in English.	☐	☐
d	He wants to write personal emails in English.	☐	☐
e	He is going to study English writing.	☐	☐

2 Types of writing

Label the types of writing with the words below.

text message   job résumé   postcard   business letter   personal letter
business email   application form   fax   personal email   diary

A

Dear Ms. Jones:

I will be in touch shortly regarding your letter of April 14.

Sincerely yours,
Evelyn Dodds

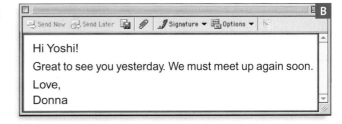

B

Hi Yoshi!
Great to see you yesterday. We must meet up again soon.
Love,
Donna

C

Dear Grandma,
   I'm writing to say thank you for the birthday card and the check. It was very kind of you to think of me.
Love,
Jamie

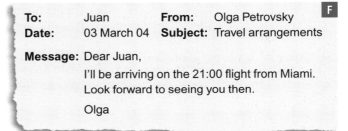

D

Chat Wa Leung

Address   2309 Eastern Parkway Los Angeles CA 90032
Qualifications   BA engineering, University of Berkeley, CA
Work Experience   3-month placement with Young & Fenwright

E

Dear John,
Thank you for coming to the meeting yesterday. It was very useful.
Regards,
Denise Edwards

F

| To: | Juan | From: | Olga Petrovsky |
| Date: | 03 March 04 | Subject: | Travel arrangements |

Message: Dear Juan,

I'll be arriving on the 21:00 flight from Miami. Look forward to seeing you then.

Olga

G

August 2004

23 Monday   Today was my first day at college! I felt a bit scared, but excited, too.

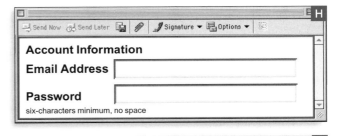

H

Account Information

Email Address [   ]

Password [   ]
six-characters minimum, no space

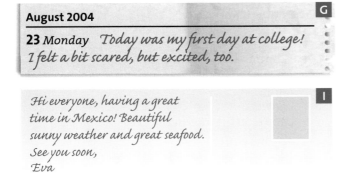

I

Hi everyone, having a great time in Mexico! Beautiful sunny weather and great seafood.
See you soon,
Eva

J

WOT RU DOING 2NITE?

3 Before you write

1 Complete these important questions with the words below.

What   Why   Who

a _____ are you writing?
e.g. to get information

b _____ are you writing to?
e.g. a friend or a stranger

c _____ are you writing?
e.g. an email or a postcard

2 **What type of correspondence would you use for each situation below? (There may be several different answers.)**

letter   text message   fax   postcard   email   greeting card

You want to …
a   ask a friend in Australia some questions about English.
(you both have computers)

_____

b   send a map and some travel information to someone.
(you made a photocopy from a magazine)

_____

c   tell a friend you are going to be late for an appointment.
(you both have cellphones)

_____

d   ask a mail-order company to send you some information.
(you have only the street address)

_____

e   congratulate a friend on a new baby.
(your friend doesn't have a computer)

_____

f   write a short message to a friend while you are on vacation.
(you don't have access to the Internet)

_____

4 A writing survey

Ask a classmate the questions below. Check (✓) the correct box or boxes for each answer, and write notes if necessary.

Writing Survey

3 Who do you write to?
friends ☐
family ☐
teachers ☐
people on the Internet ☐

Anyone else?

_____

1 Do you like writing in your own language?
yes, very much ☐
yes, it's OK ☐
no, not very much ☐
no, I don't ☐

4 How much English writing do you do?
a lot ☐
not much ☐
very little ☐
none ☐

2 What do you write in your own language?
emails ☐
letters ☐
text messages ☐
class reports ☐

Anything else?

_____

5 What types of English writing do you want to do in the future?
personal emails ☐
business emails ☐
personal letters ☐
business letters ☐

Anything else?

_____

5 Writing in your own language

1 Write a sentence about how you feel about writing in your own language.

EXAMPLE   *I like writing in my own language.*

USEFUL LANGUAGE				
I	(really)	like	…	(very much).
		don't like		

2 Write a sentence about what you write in your own language.

EXAMPLE   *I often write emails, and I occasionally send letters to my parents.*

USEFUL LANGUAGE				
I	often sometimes occasionally	write send	emails letters text messages	to my	friends. parents. teacher.
		write	reports		for my classes.

6 Writing in English

1 Write a sentence about your English writing at present.

EXAMPLE   *At present, I write a lot in English.*

USEFUL LANGUAGE		
At present,	I write a lot I don't write much I don't write anything	in English.

2 Write a sentence about types of English writing you will do in the future.

EXAMPLE   *In the future, I might write business letters in English.*

USEFUL LANGUAGE		
In the future,	I want to write … I will (probably) write … I might write …	in English.

7 Writing task

1 Look at the email on page 4. Write a similar email to your teacher.

▶ See pages 117–19 for more information about emails.

2 Introducing

IN THIS UNIT, YOU WILL ...

▶ learn how to begin and end an informal email

▶ practice making lists

▶ practice spelling and punctuation

▶ write an informal email and reply to a classmate

1 An informal email to a keypal

1 Read the email quickly. Why is Amy writing?

a to apply for a job

b to introduce herself

c to thank someone

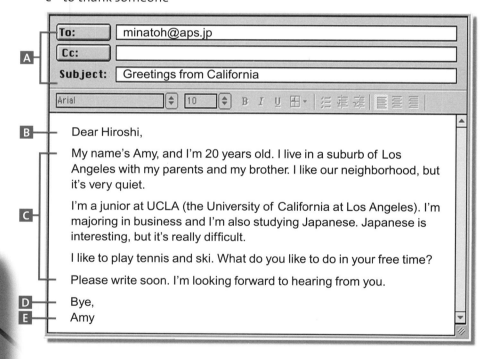

A	**To:**	minatoh@aps.jp
	Cc:	
	Subject:	Greetings from California

Arial   10   B I U

B — Dear Hiroshi,

My name's Amy, and I'm 20 years old. I live in a suburb of Los Angeles with my parents and my brother. I like our neighborhood, but it's very quiet.

C — I'm a junior at UCLA (the University of California at Los Angeles). I'm majoring in business and I'm also studying Japanese. Japanese is interesting, but it's really difficult.

I like to play tennis and ski. What do you like to do in your free time?

Please write soon. I'm looking forward to hearing from you.

D — Bye,

E — Amy

2

a _____

b _____

c _____

d _____

e _____

▶ See pages 117–19 for more information about emails.

2 Introducing yourself

1 Read the information about two young people.

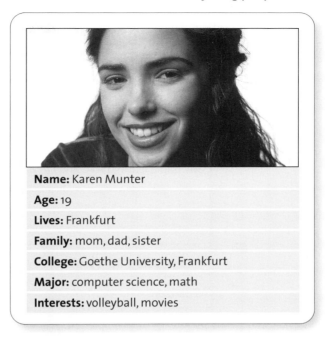

Name: Karen Munter

Age: 19

Lives: Frankfurt

Family: mom, dad, sister

College: Goethe University, Frankfurt

Major: computer science, math

Interests: volleyball, movies

Name: Emerson Piquet

Age: 21

Lives: Rio de Janeiro

Family: mom, brother

College: Rio de Janeiro State University

Major: engineering, computer science

Interests: soccer, beach volleyball

2 Read the sentences. Write "K" (Karen) or "E" (Emerson).

a I'm majoring in engineering. I'm studying computer science too. ☐
b I like to play volleyball and to go to the movies. ☐
c I'm a second year student at Goethe University in Frankfurt. ☐
d I share an apartment with my brother in Rio. ☐
e I live in Frankfurt with my mom, dad, and sister. ☐
f I'm in my third year at Rio de Janeiro State University. ☐
g I like to play soccer and beach volleyball. ☐
h I'm studying computer science and math. ☐

TIP!

You can start an informal
email with:
Dear (Jack); Hi; Hello,
and end the email with:
Bye; Bye for now; Take care

3 Write the emails from Karen and Emerson to their new keypals. Use the sentences from exercise 2 and include a closing.

To:	nikita.nabokov@mail.cis.ru
Cc:	
Subject:	Hello from Brazil

Arial 10 B *I* U ⊞ ▾ | ☰ ☲ ☲ | ☰ ☰ ☰

_____ Nikita,

My name is Emerson, and I'm 21 years old. _____

_____

_____

_____

_____

I hope to hear from you soon.

_____

Emerson

To:	w.leung@hotmail.com.cn
Cc:	
Subject:	Hi from Frankfurt

Arial 10 B *I* U ⊞ ▾ | ☰ ☲ ☲ | ☰ ☰ ☰

_____ Wae-ling,

My name's Karen, and I'm 19 years old. _____

_____

_____

_____

_____

Write soon!

_____

Karen

3 Listing main points

Before Amy sent her email to Hiroshi, she wrote a list of main points.

1	home	LA – suburbs – quiet neighborhood
2	family	mother, father, one brother
3	college	UCLA – Business major – Japanese
4	interests	tennis, skiing

Write notes about yourself, using the same headings.

home

family

college

interests

4 Spot the mistake

1 **Rewrite the sentences with the correct punctuation and capitalization.**

   a are you interested in art

   b school starts in april

   c im a second-year student

   d my brothers name is ken

2 **Rewrite the sentences with the correct spelling.**

   a I live in the subarbs.

   b It's a teriffic place.

   c Have you tryed para-gliding?

   d The wether here is beautiful right now.

   ▶ See pages 119–23 for more information about spelling and punctuation.

5 Asking questions

1 **Complete the sentences using the words below.**

   actor   pets   weekends   kick-boxing   dish   musical instrument

   a What do you like to do on _____?
   b What's your favorite _____ ?
   c Who's your favorite _____ ?
   d Are you interested in _____ ?
   e Do you play a _____ ?
   f Do you have any _____ ?

2 **Work with a partner. Take turns to ask each other the questions.**

6 A reply to a keypal's email

Look at Hiroshi's reply to Amy's email. There are three spelling mistakes, two punctuation mistakes, and one capitalization mistake. There is also one sentence that is in the wrong place. Correct the mistakes, and rewrite the email.

To: amydexter@mac.com
Cc:
Subject: Thank you

Arial | 10 | B I U

Dear amy,

Thanks very much for your email and the foto.

I'm 19 years old. I live in Kichijoji, a suburb of Tokyo.

Im a freshman at Tokai University in Tokyo. My major is sociology, and I'm also studing Spanish.

I love flamenco music. What kind of music do you like!

I also like sports, and I sometimes go swiming at the local sports club.

The attachment is a photo of me and my guitar. I like Spanish, but the grammar is difficult.

Keep in touch.

Bye,

Hiroshi

me and my guitar

7 Writing task

1   Find one classmate to be your new keypal. Write down his or her name and email address. Try to find someone you don't know well.

2   Write a short email to your new keypal. Use true information about yourself. Remember to ask some questions too!

REMEMBER!

Always check your writing. Think about:
— **Why** you are writing (e.g. self-introduction: give factual information about you)
— **Who** you are writing to (e.g. classmate: informal greeting and closing)
— **What** you are writing (e.g. email: include a subject to describe your message)

USEFUL LANGUAGE

I'm a	freshman junior/sophomore/senior first-year student	at	Dong-A University.
My major is I'm studying	biology. modern languages.		
I live	in (a suburb of)		Busan.
	near		
I have	one brother and two sisters.		
I don't have	any brothers or sisters.		
I like	hip-hop.		
	to play soccer.		

3   Exchange emails with your keypal and write a reply. Start like this:

Dear David,
Thanks for your email …

3 Completing forms

▶ complete forms by hand

▶ complete forms on the Internet

▶ use capital letters

1 Two forms

1 Read forms A and B quickly. Write "A" or "B" for each question.

a Which form is
1 a check-in form for a hotel? ☐
2 an application form for a language course? ☐

b Which form was filled out
1 on a computer? ☐
2 by hand? ☐

FORM A

Partridge University Texas

Summer English Program

Application Form

Instructions: Please complete this form and then click the 'Submit' button below.

Need help? Please email us: internationalcenter@partridge.edu

Contact Information

Family Name	Ruiz
First Name	Carmen
Gender	○ Male ● Female
Email Address	bananas@hotmail.com
Mailing Address	Calle 7 de Majo 2223
City	Buenos Aires
Country	Argentina
Zip Code	C1008BBX
Phone number	+54 (11) 4461 5770

(Submit)

TOWER HOTEL · HONOLULU

Date *09/07/04*   Number of nights: *2*
Family Name   *YOON*
First Name   *IN-JUNG*
Mailing Address *33-4 NONHYON-DONG, KANGNAM-KU*
City   *SEOUL*
Country   *SOUTH KOREA*
Zip Code   *135-010*
Phone number   *+82 (2)624-7139*

2 Now answer the questions.

   a What is Carmen's family name?
   b Which city does she come from?
   c Which hotel is In-Jung staying at?
   d How long is he going to stay?
   e Where is he from?

3 What are some other situations in which you fill out a form by hand or on a computer? Discuss them with your partner.

2 Filling out a form by hand

REMEMBER!

CAPITALS are *upper-case* letters, e.g. ABC.

The opposite of *upper-case* letters is *lower-case*, e.g. abc.

You may see the following instructions for completing forms by hand:
Please complete in BLOCK CAPITALS.
Please print in CAPITAL LETTERS.

Both sentences mean to write words without joining the letters, and using capital letters only.

1 When you visit the U.S. as a tourist, student, or businessperson, you must fill out an I-94 form. Look at the first part (Arrival Record) of the form on the next page. Underline the words (a–e) in the instructions.

   a completed
   b print
   c legibly
   d capital
   e present

2 Now match the words from exercise 1 with these definitions.

   1 write letters without joining ☐
   2 filled out ☐
   3 give ☐
   4 clearly ☐
   5 upper case ☐

3 Are these statements about the instructions true (T) or false (F)? Check (✓) the correct box.

When you complete the form, you …	T	F
a must write clearly.	☐	☐
b can use a pencil.	☐	☐
c can write in lower-case letters.	☐	☐
d must use English.	☐	☐
e must complete both parts of the form.	☐	☐

I-94 Arrival/Departure Record - Instructions

This form must be completed by all persons except U.S. citizens, returning resident aliens, aliens with immigrant visas, and Canadian Citizens visiting or in transit.

Type or print legibly with pen in ALL CAPITAL LETTERS. Use English. Do not write on the back of this form.

This form is in two parts. Please complete both the Arrival Record (items 1 through 13) and the Departure Record (items 14 through 17).

When all items are completed, present this form to the U.S. Immigration and Naturalization service Inspector.

Item 7 – If you are entering the United Sates by land, enter LAND in this space. If you are entering the United Sates by ship, enter SEA in this space.

Admission Number

411993827 07

Immigration and
Naturalization Service

1-94
Arrival Record

1 Family Name
W A T A N A B E

2 First (Given) Name	3 Birth Date (Mo/Day/Yr)
K E I K O	0 3 0 7 8 2

4 Country of Citizenship	5 Sex (Male or Female)
J A P A N	F E M A L E

6 Passport Number	7 Airline and Flight Number
W B 4 2 2 5 1 0 2	J A L 9 2 9

8 Country Where You Live	9 City Where You Boarded
J A P A N	T O K Y O

10 City Where Visa Was Issued	11 Date Issued (Mo/Day/Yr)
T O K Y O	0 1 2 2 0 2

12 Address While in the United States (Number and Street)
3 3 9   B O N D   S T

13 City and State
N E W   Y O R K   N Y   1 0 0 1 2

4   Now answer the questions.

a   What's Keiko's family name?

It's _____

b   In which month was she born?

She was born in _____

c   Where does she live?

She lives in _____

d   In which city did she get on the plane?

She got on in _____

e   Where is she staying in the U.S.?

At _____

3 Writing task 1

Fill out the first part of the I-94 using your own ideas and / or the information on the right.

Flight – AA7230
Kansai International Airport
(Osaka) to Los Angeles
US Address – 116779 Boulder Ave.
La Mirada, CA 90638

Admission Number

411993955 04

Immigration and
Naturalization Service

1-94
Arrival Record

1 Family Name

2 First (Given) Name | 3 Birth Date (Mo/Day/Yr)

4 Country of Citizenship | 5 Sex (Male or Female)

6 Passport Number | 7 Airline and Flight Number

8 Country Where You Live | 9 City Where You Boarded

10 City Where Visa Was Issued | 11 Date Issued (Mo/Day/Yr)

12 Address While in the United States (Number and Street)

13 City and State

4 Registering online

1 Check (✓) the Internet services you have registered for in your own language (L1) and in English (Eng).

shopping website   software   other
email account   information website

L1

Eng

2 Work with a partner. Take turns asking and answering about registering for Internet services, like this:

A: *Have you ever registered for an Internet service?*
B: *Yes, I have.*
A: *What kind?*
B: *A shopping website – Mandarin Computer. I bought a laptop.*
A: *Did you register in English?*
B: *No, I didn't.*

3 Read the Hotmail application form quickly.

a How many times do you have to write your password?

b How many secret questions do you have to answer?

c Which characters do you have to type for a registration check?

First name	Stacey
Last name	Rivers

Your first and last names will be sent with all outgoing e-mail messages.

Language	English
Country/Region	United States
State	Arizona
ZIP Code	85701
Time Zone	Arizona - MST
Gender	○ Male ● Female
Birth Date	March 10 1985 (ex. 1999)
Occupation	Accounting/Finance

Account Information

Email Address	srivers @hotmail.com
Password six-characters minimum; no spaces	******
Retype Password	******
Secret Question	Favorite pet's name?
Secret Answer	********
Alternate E-mail Address (optional)	staceyrivers@yahoo.com
Registration Check	Type the characters that you see in this picture.

A 6 7 E J P 4

a67ejp4

Characters are not case-sensitive.

4 Are these statements true (T) or false (F)? Check (✓) the correct box.

	T	F
a Stacey wants a Hotmail account in English.	☐	☐
b She lives in California.	☐	☐
c She's a teacher.	☐	☐
d She was born in 1981.	☐	☐
e Stacey's password is *maplesyrup*.	☐	☐
f Her secret question is about her pet.	☐	☐

5 Writing Task 2

Register for an English email account. Your teacher will give you some URLs to choose from if you need help. If you do not have access to a computer in class, complete the registration form below.

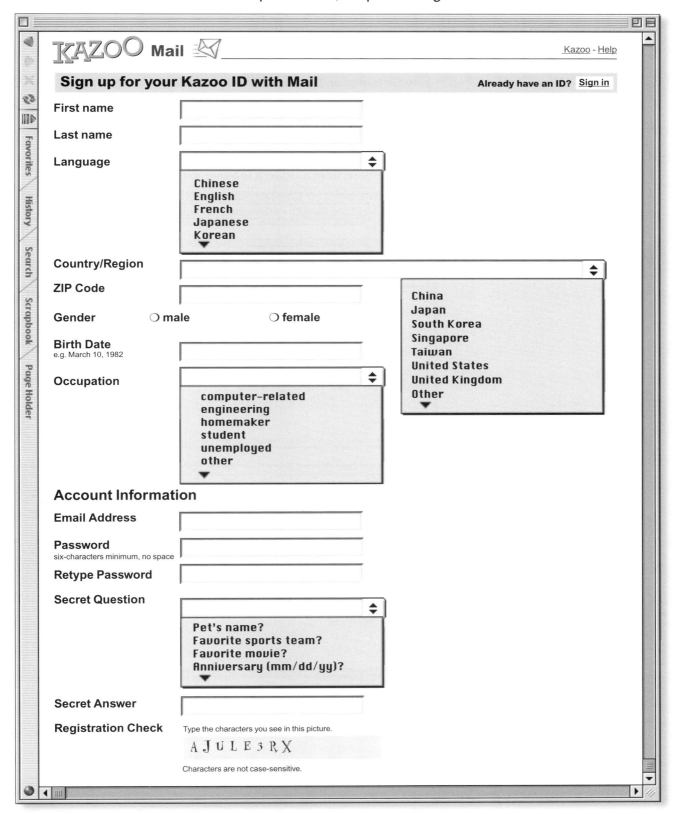

KAZOO Mail

Kazoo - Help

Sign up for your Kazoo ID with Mail

Already have an ID? Sign in

First name

Last name

Language

Chinese
English
French
Japanese
Korean

Country/Region

ZIP Code

China
Japan
South Korea
Singapore
Taiwan
United States
United Kingdom
Other

Gender ○ male   ○ female

Birth Date
e.g. March 10, 1982

Occupation

computer-related
engineering
homemaker
student
unemployed
other

Account Information

Email Address

Password
six-characters minimum, no space

Retype Password

Secret Question

Pet's name?
Favorite sports team?
Favorite movie?
Anniversary (mm/dd/yy)?

Secret Answer

Registration Check   Type the characters you see in this picture.

A J U L E 3 R X

Characters are not case-sensitive.

4 Thanking

IN THIS UNIT, YOU WILL LEARN HOW TO ...

▶ write formal and informal thank-you emails

▶ recognize and use formal and informal writing styles

1 Two emails

1 Read the emails from a student in Singapore.

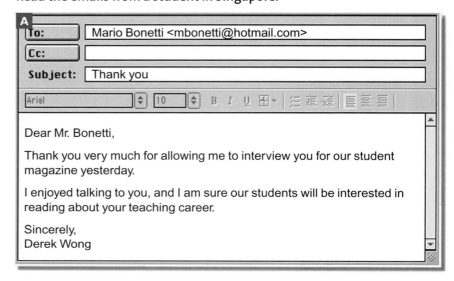

A

To:	Mario Bonetti <mbonetti@hotmail.com>
Cc:	
Subject:	Thank you

Arial · 10 · B I U ⊞· ⋮≡ ≣ ≣ | ≣ ≣ ≣ |

Dear Mr. Bonetti,

Thank you very much for allowing me to interview you for our student magazine yesterday.

I enjoyed talking to you, and I am sure our students will be interested in reading about your teaching career.

Sincerely,
Derek Wong

B

To:	Gina Minardi <gminardi@pacific.net.sg>
Cc:	
Subject:	Thanks

Arial · 10 · B I U ⊞· ⋮≡ ≣ ≣ | ≣ ≣ ≣ |

Gina,

Working hard at the moment - how about you? Thanks for looking at my report - great help! :-)

See you,
Derek

2 Check (✓) one or two boxes for each question.

Which email is ...   A   B
a   to Derek's friend?   ☐   ☐
b   to a teacher at Derek's school?   ☐   ☐
c   thanking for something?   ☐   ☐
d   formal?   ☐   ☐
e   informal?   ☐   ☐

2 Formal or informal?

Would you write a formal or an informal email in each situation below? Check (✓) one box for each situation.

	You want to …	formal	informal
a	thank a friend for a gift.	☐	☐
b	apply for a job.	☐	☐
c	ask a language school about courses.	☐	☐
d	ask a friend about his / her new job.	☐	☐
e	write to a company to complain about a product.	☐	☐

3 Salutations

1 Look at some differences between formal and informal salutations and closings.

> **LANGUAGE FOCUS**
>
> Salutations and closings are different for formal and informal emails:
>
> | FORMAL | | INFORMAL |
> |---|---|---|
> | Dear | Sir / Madam, | Dear Sarah, |
> | | Mr. / Ms. Black, | Hi, |
> | | Dr. Mitchell, | Hello John, |
> | Sincerely yours, | | Bye, |
> | Sincerely, | | See you, |
> | | | Take care, |

▶ See pages 117–18 for more information about salutations and closings.

2 Write a formal salutation for each of these people.

a Henry Andersson

_____

b Mary Ford, a medical doctor

_____

c Gina Davis

_____

d Jun Hasegawa, a university professor

_____

3 Now imagine the people in exercise 1 are your friends. Write an informal salutation for each of them.

a _____

b _____

c _____

d _____

4 Closings

1 Read these closings. Write "F" (formal) or "I" (informal) for each one.

a Sincerely,
  Pablo Suarez   _____

d *Take care,*
  Jacques   _____

b WbW,
  Annie   _____

e Bye,
  Vicky ;-)   _____

c *Sincerely yours,*
  Vittorio Morelli   _____

f Yours truly,
  Henrik Andersson   _____

▶ See page 129 for more information about email abbreviations and text messaging language.

2 Write two formal and two informal closings using your own name.

formal	informal
_____	_____
_____	_____
_____	_____
_____	_____

5 Formal and informal writing styles

REMEMBER!

There are other differences between formal and informal writing, e.g. formal sentences are sometimes longer and more complex; informal sentences are sometimes shorter and simpler.

1

LANGUAGE FOCUS

Look at some differences between formal and informal correspondence:

FORMAL	INFORMAL
complete sentences	incomplete sentences, e.g. omission of verb subject (*I, you*), auxiliary verb (*am, have*)
no contractions	use of contractions (*I'm, you're*)
regular punctuation	expressive punctuation, e.g. exclamation points (!)
no text messaging abbreviations or emoticons	text messaging abbreviations and emoticons

Work with a partner. Look at the emails on page 20. Can you find an example of each item from the table above?

TIP!

Here are some common email / text-messaging abbreviations:

CUL8R = see you later
WbW = with best wishes
FYI = for your information
BTW = by the way

2 Read these pairs of sentences. Write "F" (formal) or "I" (informal) for each sentence.

a Everything OK? ☐
b I hope you are well. ☐

c Thank you for your letter of September 5, 2004. ☐
d Got your letter the other day – thanks! ☐

e Perhaps you could call me at your convenience? ☐
f Give me a ring sometime, OK? ☐

g I've sent you an attachment. ☐
h I have attached a file for your information. ☐

i I look forward to hearing from you soon. ☐
j Can't wait to hear your news!! ☐

k CUL8R, ☐
l Best wishes, ☐

3 Match each description below (1–5) with one or more sentences from exercise 2.

1 a contraction _____
2 an incomplete sentence _____
3 regular punctuation _____
4 expressive punctuation _____
5 a text-messaging abbreviation _____

6 Thanking

1 Write the formal and informal phrases in the correct position in the chart below.

Thanks   Thanks a lot
Thank you very much   I am writing to thank you

formal	a _____	for helping me with my report. I learned a great deal.
	b _____	
informal	c _____	for helping me with my report. You were terrific!
	d _____	

2 Read the email from an English language student, Vladimir Malevich, to his teacher, Cindy McNally. Work with a partner, and rewrite the email in a more formal style.

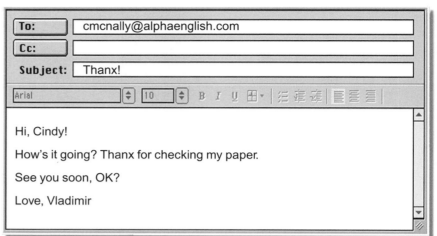

To: cmcnally@alphaenglish.com
Cc:
Subject: Thanx!

Arial   10   B I U

Hi, Cindy!

How's it going? Thanx for checking my paper.

See you soon, OK?

Love, Vladimir

3 Read the email from another language student, Anna Vargas, to her good friend, Shiro Watanabe. Work with a partner, and rewrite the email in a more informal style. When you have finished, compare your emails with another pair of students.

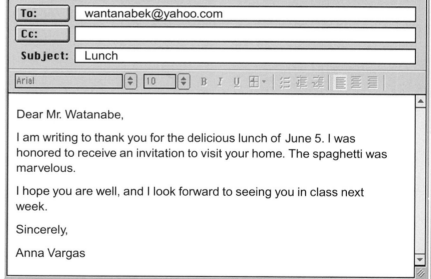

To: wantanabek@yahoo.com
Cc:
Subject: Lunch

Arial   10   B I U

Dear Mr. Watanabe,

I am writing to thank you for the delicious lunch of June 5. I was honored to receive an invitation to visit your home. The spaghetti was marvelous.

I hope you are well, and I look forward to seeing you in class next week.

Sincerely,

Anna Vargas

7 Writing task 1

Choose one of the situations below, and write a formal email to thank someone you don't know well (think of a name). You can use the ideas below and / or your own ideas.

He / She ...

invited you to a party.
— you enjoyed it very much
— everyone was very friendly

gave you a ride home.
— it was a great help
— you hope your friend got home safely

invited you to dinner.
— it was delicious
— what was the name of the dessert?

lent you some DVDs.
— they were very interesting
— you'll give them back very soon

8 Writing task 2

Choose one more situation in exercise 7, and write an informal email to thank a friend (think of a name).

5 Requesting information

1 A letter

1 Read the letter from a student in Mexico.

Calle 5 de Majo 52
Hipodromo
Condesa
Mexico DF
Mexico

Home and Away
475 Western Avenue
Melbourne 3001
Victoria
Australia

October 6, 2004

Dear Home and Away:

I am hoping to visit Australia later this year, and I recently saw your advertisement about homestay programs in "International Student" magazine.

Could you please send me a copy of your latest catalog?

I look forward to hearing from you.

Sincerely,

Maria Rivera

Maria Rivera

2 Answer the questions.

a Which company is Maria writing to?
b Why doesn't she write a person's name in the salutation?
c In which magazine did she see the advertisement?
d What does she ask the company to do?

2 Organizing a letter

Look at these parts of a letter to an art school in Washington. Write them in the correct position in the letter on page 28.

Would you please send me your latest catalog and tuition details?

Thank you in advance for your help.

Dear Sir or Madam,

Jiro Tanizaki

Amanuma
Kawagoe-ku 5
Saitama 350-1224
Japan

Radcliffe College of Art
1500 28th St. NE
Washington, D.C. 20018
USA

I am thinking of studying digital media design in the U.S., and I was interested in your advertisement in a recent issue of "Art in America" magazine.

Jiro Tanizaki

Sincerely yours,

February 6, 2004

(blank lined letter template)

► See pages 109–11 for more information about the layout of a letter.

3 Salutations

Publicity
Department

Personnel Manager

LANGUAGE FOCUS

If you are writing a business email to an organization, or someone whose name you don't know, you can use these salutations:

Dear Sir or Madam,
the person's job title: _Dear Advertising Manager,_
the name of the department: _Dear Personnel Department,_
the name of the company: _Dear Apple Computer,_

Write four salutations, using your own ideas and / or the ideas on the left.

a _____
b _____
c _____
d _____

► See pages 117–18 for more information about salutations.

4 Giving a reason

1 Write the correct sentence (1–4) below the matching picture.

1 I am a Computer Studies student at Taipei University.
2 I would like to pursue a career as a flight attendant.
3 I am planning to travel in Europe next summer.
4 I am thinking of studying French in Paris this summer.

2 Write the phrases in each sentence in the correct order.

a in the *Straits Times*. / your advertisement / I saw /
for intensive courses

_____

b on your website. / the group tours / I'm very interested in

_____

c your new security software / I was very interested to /
in *Time* magazine. / read about

_____

d I was interested in / on your website. / the jobs

_____

3 Now join the matching sentences in exercises 1 and 2 like this:

a *I am thinking of studying French in Paris this summer, and I saw your advertisement for intensive courses in the "Straits Times".*

b _____

_____

c _____

_____

d _____

_____

5 Requesting information

To ask someone (a company, school, etc.) to do something, you can use these forms:

USEFUL LANGUAGE		
Could Would	you please send me	some information about your products? a course catalog?
Please send me		your latest catalog. information about your course.

Write requests for these situations. Use all three forms. You want …

a a travel agency to send you their latest brochure.

_____

_____

_____

b a university to send you their course catalog.

_____

_____

_____

c a language school to send you details of their English courses.

_____

_____

_____

d a computer software company to send you information about their products.

_____

_____

_____

6 Writing a conclusion

Check (✓) the sentences you think are concluding sentences.

a I saw your advertisement in the *Buenos Aires Herald*. ☐
b I hope to hear from you soon. ☐
c I am a business studies student at Oxford University. ☐
d I am writing to thank you for the lovely birthday present. ☐
e I look forward to hearing from you. ☐
f Thank you in advance for your help. ☐

7 Writing tasks

1 Choose one of the items below and write a letter requesting information. Include a salutation, introduction, reason, request, concluding sentence, closing (for example, *Sincerely,*) and your name.

▶ See pages 117–18 for more information about closings.

online MBA

The No. 1 choice for your business education

For information:
admissions@Kellogcollege.ac.uk

WESTERFIELD INSTITUTE
Brookville ME 00821

You can understand economics!

Ten-lesson course
Tuition free – small charge for materials

BTC
Bard Theater Company
Open-air performances of Shakespeare's plays in July and August
For further details, contact us at www.bardtheater.com

OXMINSTER
UNIVERSITY PRESS

You need **Workplace** – the new textbook that prepares students for using English at work.

For more information, please contact us at elt.enquiry@oxmin.co.uk

2 Find a school, company or organization that interests you, and write a letter asking for information. For ideas, look at advertisements on the Internet, in magazines, or in newspapers.

Review 1

1 Writing to a keypal

1 Read this email from Amy to her keypal Hiroshi. What is her main purpose for writing? Check (✓) the right answer.

a She wants Hiroshi to do something for her. ☐
b She is just being friendly. ☐
c She is inviting Hiroshi to go to the movies. ☐

To:	Hiroshi <minatoh@aps.jp>
Cc:	
Subject:	hello

Arial   10   B I U ⊞▾ ⋮☰ ⫷⫸ ☰☰☰

Hi Hiroshi,

How are you? I'm pretty good, but I'm very busy with school work. In fact, I'd like to ask you a favor. My film class is studying movies from different cultures. Each student has to choose a country to study. Of course I chose Japan! But I don't know much about this subject. Can you tell me the names of some popular movies?

By the way, what kind of movies do you like?

I'll write again when I have more time.

Bye for now,
Amy

2 Read Hiroshi's answer to Amy. There are three mistakes in his letter (punctuation, capitalization, and spelling). ⟨Circle⟩ each mistake.

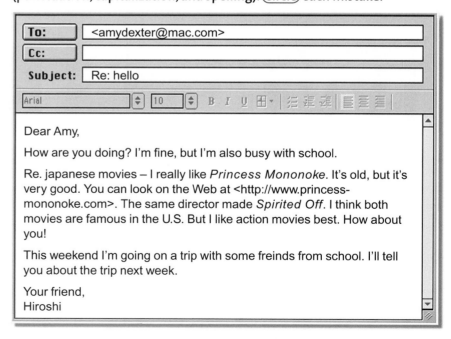

To:	<amydexter@mac.com>
Cc:	
Subject:	Re: hello

Arial   10   B I U ⊞▾ ⋮☰ ⫷⫸ ☰☰☰

Dear Amy,

How are you doing? I'm fine, but I'm also busy with school.

Re. japanese movies – I really like *Princess Mononoke*. It's old, but it's very good. You can look on the Web at <http://www.princess-mononoke.com>. The same director made *Spirited Off*. I think both movies are famous in the U.S. But I like action movies best. How about you!

This weekend I'm going on a trip with some freinds from school. I'll tell you about the trip next week.

Your friend,
Hiroshi

3 Now correct Hiroshi's mistakes. Write the complete corrected sentences below.

a _____

b _____

c _____

4 After Amy received Hiroshi's reply, she wrote to him again. Complete her paragraphs by writing the missing sentences from the list below.

a   I don't like action movies very much, though.
b   What's the name in Japanese?
c   I'm looking forward to hearing about it.
d   Thanks a lot for your help!

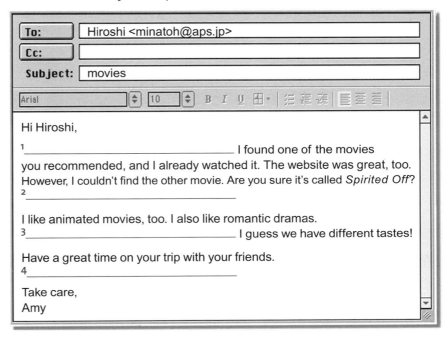

To: Hiroshi <minatoh@aps.jp>
Cc:
Subject: movies

Arial   10   B I U ⊞▾ ⌘ ⌘ ⌘ ⌘ ⌘ ⌘

Hi Hiroshi,

1_____ I found one of the movies you recommended, and I already watched it. The website was great, too. However, I couldn't find the other movie. Are you sure it's called *Spirited Off*?
2_____

I like animated movies, too. I also like romantic dramas.
3_____ I guess we have different tastes!

Have a great time on your trip with your friends.
4_____

Take care,
Amy

2 Completing forms

Fill out the form below. Use your own information. Imagine that your address in London is the Pleasant Inn Hotel, 20 Lime Walk, London W2 3EG.

LANDING CARD
Immigration Act 1971

Please complete clearly in BLOCK CAPITALS

Family name ....

Forenames ....   Sex (M,F) ⊔⊔

Date of birth (Day Month Year) ⊔ ⊔ ⊔ ⊔ ⊔ ⊔

Nationality ....   Occupation ....

Address in United Kingdom ....

....

Signature ....   **AFL 28 992**

for Official use
CAT ☐   18 ☐   CODE ☐   NAT ☐   POL ☐

3 Formal or informal?

Read the salutation or closing for each letter. Decide if it is formal or informal. Then write the appropriate sentence (a or b) on each line.

1 Dear Professor Lee,

_____

  a Hi! How's it going?
  b I am pleased to be in your writing class this term.

2 Dear Admissions Office,

_____

  a I would like to enroll in your summer English program.
  b Hello! My name's Susan.

3 Hi Kim!

_____

  a It was a pleasure seeing you again the other day.
  b Great to see you yesterday!

4 _____
Sincerely yours,
David Bourne
  a Thanks for everything!
  b Thank you very much for all your help.

5 _____
See ya tomorrow–
Terri
  a Could you please let me know the cost of a ticket?
  b How much do the tickets cost?

4 Pairwork dictation

1 Work with a partner. Take turns reading sentences to your partner, who will write them down. Student A, use the sentences on page 105. Student B, use the sentences on page 106.

USEFUL LANGUAGE

Could you say that again?
Could you speak more slowly?
How do you spell "…"?
What's the (fourth) word?

Now, write the sentences that your partner reads:

a _____

b _____

c _____

d _____

e _____

f _____

2 When you are finished, compare your sentences with your partner's page. Did you write everything correctly?

5 Word puzzle

Write the answers to the clues below in the puzzle. When you are finished, read down to find the answer to this question:

What type of salutation is *Dear Sir or Madam*?

a To join a club, you fill out an application f_____ .

b You need a p_____ for your email account.

c A common closing is S_____ .

d A course catalog gives i_____ about a school or university.

e The first word of a common salutation is d_____ .

f Please write your first name and your l_____ name.

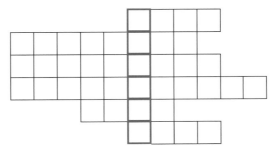

6 Writing and culture: short cuts

TIP!

You can use abbreviations (like NY for New York) or emoticons (like :-(to show you are unhappy) to write more quickly or send shorter messages. These are not appropriate for formal emails, but are common among friends or for informal messages.

1 Read the email below. How many abbreviations and emoticons are there? Circle them.

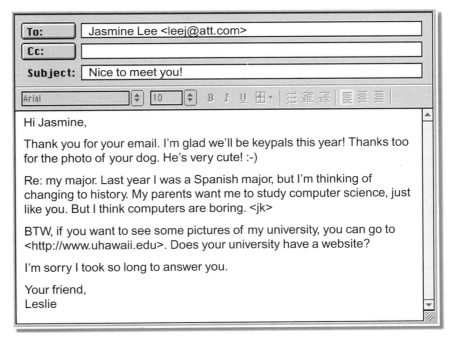

To: Jasmine Lee <leej@att.com>

Cc:

Subject: Nice to meet you!

Hi Jasmine,

Thank you for your email. I'm glad we'll be keypals this year! Thanks too for the photo of your dog. He's very cute! :-)

Re: my major. Last year I was a Spanish major, but I'm thinking of changing to history. My parents want me to study computer science, just like you. But I think computers are boring. <jk>

BTW, if you want to see some pictures of my university, you can go to <http://www.uhawaii.edu>. Does your university have a website?

I'm sorry I took so long to answer you.

Your friend,
Leslie

2 Match each abbreviation and emoticon to its meaning.

a :-)   1 just kidding

b ASAP   2 happy

c Re: 3 by the way (to change the subject)

d <jk>   4 wink

e BTW   5 this is about / in reference to

f ;-)   6 as soon as possible

6 Getting details

1 An email to a host family

1 Read the email to a host family in Oregon quickly. What is Kurt's main reason for writing to Mr. and Mrs. Polanski?

a   to ask if he can visit them
b   to answer their questions
c   to ask for some information

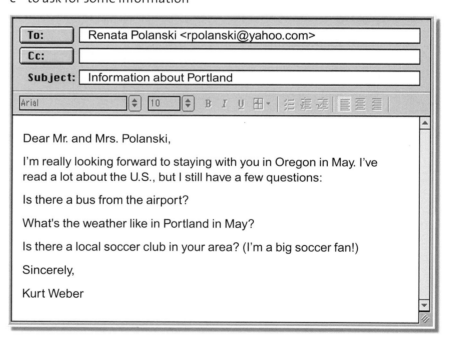

To:	Renata Polanski <rpolanski@yahoo.com>
Cc:	
Subject:	Information about Portland

Arial   10   B I U ⊞ ▾ ⁞ ⁞ ⁞ ⁞ ⁞ ⁞ ⁞

Dear Mr. and Mrs. Polanski,

I'm really looking forward to staying with you in Oregon in May. I've read a lot about the U.S., but I still have a few questions:

Is there a bus from the airport?

What's the weather like in Portland in May?

Is there a local soccer club in your area? (I'm a big soccer fan!)

Sincerely,

Kurt Weber

2 Now answer the questions.

a   Is Kurt going to visit Oregon?
b   Has he read much about the U.S.?
c   Does he ask about the weather?
d   Does he ask about food?
e   Is he an American football fan?

2 Appropriate questions

Which of these questions can you ask in an email to a host family before your first visit? Mark each one ✓ (OK), ✗ (not OK), or ? (possible).

a Is your house clean? ☐
b Can I cook my own meals? ☐
c Can you help me with my English if I have problems? ☐
d Do you have any pets? ☐
e Is it safe to walk alone at night in your neighborhood? ☐
f What is your religion? ☐
g Can I use your car? ☐
h What do you think of the political situation in your country? ☐
i Do you have a computer that I can use for email? ☐
j Can I take a weekend trip? ☐

2 **Compare your answers with a partner. Then write two appropriate questions of your own.**

3 Question forms

1

<table>
<tr><td colspan="3">**LANGUAGE FOCUS**</td></tr>
</table>

There are two main types of questions:

Yes / no questions	*Is the weather warm in spring?*	*Yes, it is.*
	Do you ever eat pasta at home?	*No, I don't.*
Wh- questions	*What's the weather like in spring?*	*It's hot!*
	What type of food do you eat at home?	*We usually eat fish and rice.*

Write *yes / no* questions and answers.

You want to know if …

it is safe to walk alone at night. ✓
Is it safe to walk alone at night?   *Yes, it is.*

the family has a computer ✗
Do you have a computer?   *No, we don't.*

a it is OK to smoke in the house. ✗

_____

b you need to bring warm clothes. ✓

_____

c there is a swimming pool in the neighborhood. ✗

_____

d you can use the local library. ✓

_____

e there are bars in the area. ✗

_____

2 Read the answers. Then write appropriate *wh-* questions, e.g.

You should take the number 21 bus.
Which bus should I take?

a The last train is at 11:30 p.m.

When is _____ .

b You can play tennis at the local sports center.

Where can _____

c You should bring warm clothes.

What type of clothes should _____

d You should see Mrs. Laker at the Laker School of English about classes.

Who should _____

e You need an International Driver's License to rent a car.

What do I need _____

4 Your email to a host family

1 You are going to visit a foreign country for the first time and stay with a host family. Choose one of the families below, or use your own ideas.

family	Patel	Voller	Cooper
country	UK	Canada	New Zealand
city	Oxford	Ottawa	Wellington
season	spring	summer	fall

2 Write some questions (*yes / no* and *wh-*) to ask your host family. Use the ideas below to help you.

_____

_____

_____

transportation   weather   safety
your room   entertainment   sports facilities
language schools   help with English food

5 Writing task 1

Write a short email to your host family. You can use Kurt's email in exercise 1.1 to help you.

6 Replying to questions

1 When you reply to another email, you can:
— create a new email message
— use the reply function, and include all of the other email
— use the reply function, and include some of the other email.

Note: When you use the reply function, the subject line automatically changes to *Re: + original title* (*Re: =* about, concerning, in reference to)

2 Read Mrs. Polanski's reply to Kurt. Which method in exercise 1 does she use?

To: Kurt Weber <kweber@yahoo.com.de>

Cc:

Subject: Re: Information about Portland

Arial   10   B *I* U ⊞▾ | ≣ ≣ ≣ | ≣ ≣ ≣

Dear Kurt,

Thank you for your email. We are looking forward to your visit, too.

Here are some answers to your questions:

> Is there a bus from the airport?

Yes, there are buses to the city center every 30 minutes, but we'll pick you up at the airport, so don't worry.

> What's the weather like in Portland in May?

It's usually very pleasant, around 65°F – that's 18°c, I think!

> Is there a local soccer club in your area? (I'm a big soccer fan!)

No, I'm sorry, there isn't a local club near us.

I hope this helps. If you have any more questions, please ask!

Best regards,

Renata Polanski

---

3 Are these statements true (T) or false (F)? Check (✓) the correct box.

		T	F
a	You can get a bus from the airport to the city center.	☐	☐
b	Kurt will take a bus from the airport.	☐	☐
c	Kurt won't need a thick sweater.	☐	☐
d	There is a local soccer club in Portland.	☐	☐

7 Answering questions

1 Match the questions on the left with the answers on the right.

a How much does it cost to eat out?

b What clothes should I bring for the summer?

c Is there somewhere I can play tennis in your neighborhood?

d Do young people hitchhike in your country?

e How much money will I need per week?

f Can I rent a bike easily?

g What's the best way to get to your place from the airport?

h Is it expensive to rent a car?

1 Make sure you bring lots of T-shirts; it's hot!

2 A good three-course meal costs about $20.

3 Yes. Mountain bikes are cheap.

4 I recommend you take the subway.

5 Yes, you can play at the public courts for $3 an hour.

6 It's about $50 a day at Autorent.

7 Bring about $300.

8 Some people do, but I don't recommend it. It's dangerous.

2 Imagine the questions in exercise 1 are about the town or city where you live. Work with a partner, and write replies for the questions.

USEFUL LANGUAGE	
You can	rent a bike from a store in town. get a meal for about $20. play at the local tennis court.
I recommend you Make sure you	take the subway. get travel insurance.
Bring You'll need	your sun hat! about $300 a week.
I don't recommend you It's not a good idea to	hitchhike. carry too much cash.
Be careful of	pickpockets. strangers who are too friendly.

EXAMPLE How much does it cost to eat out?
You can get a meal for two people, including wine, for about $50.

_____

_____

_____

_____

_____

3 Compare your replies with another pair of students.

8 Writing task 2

1 Find a partner who comes from a different town or city. Imagine that you are a foreign student who is going to stay with his / her family.

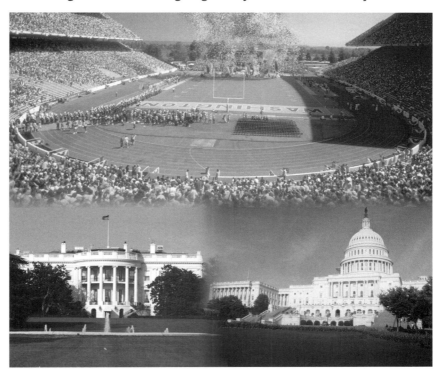

> Write an email to your host family asking for information about their town or city. Remember to use *yes / no* and *wh-* questions.

> Send your email to your partner.

2 Now imagine you are a member of the host family.

> Read the email from your partner.

> Write a reply to the email, answering your partner's questions. Use the message reply function.

> Send your email to your partner.

3 Try to find a classmate who asked for information about the same town or city. Compare the questions you asked and the answers you received.

7 Inviting and arranging to meet

► write an invitation

► suggest when and where to meet

► accept and refuse an invitation

► write days, dates, and times

► use the present continuous and simple present tenses

► write about the future

1 An invitation

1 Read the email from a young American woman to a Colombian friend.

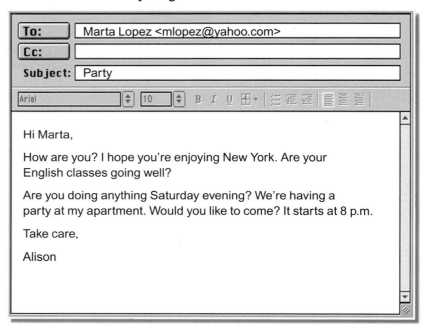

To: Marta Lopez <mlopez@yahoo.com>

Cc:

Subject: Party

Arial 10 B *I* U

Hi Marta,

How are you? I hope you're enjoying New York. Are your English classes going well?

Are you doing anything Saturday evening? We're having a party at my apartment. Would you like to come? It starts at 8 p.m.

Take care,

Alison

2 Complete the sentences using the question words below.

What   Why   Who   Where   When

a _____ is Alison writing to?   To Marta.

b _____ is Marta staying?   In New York.

c _____ is she doing there?   She's studying English.

d _____ is Alison writing?   To invite Marta to a party.

e _____ does the party start?   At 8:00.

2 Talking about the future

1

We can use the present continuous tense for:

actions that are happening now
What's Jane doing? She's watching TV.

future arrangements
What are you doing this weekend?
We're going to Boston.

Look at the email in 1.1 again. Alison uses the present continuous tense to write about what is happening right now. Write one of the sentences.

a _____

Alison also uses the present continuous tense to write about the future. Write one of the sentences.

b _____

2 Read the sentences. Write "P" (Present) or "F" (Future) in the boxes.

a What time are you meeting Zoltán? ☐
b Sorry, I can't make it on Sunday. I'm playing tennis with Jeff. ☐
c I'm writing this in my favorite coffee shop. ☐
d Are you doing anything special on Thursday? ☐
e Maria's working out at the sports club right now. ☐

3

We can use the simple present tense to talk about timetables and schedules:

When does the flight leave tomorrow?
It leaves at 11:20 a.m.
How long is the concert?
It starts at 7:30 p.m. and finishes at 9 p.m.

Complete the sentences using the simple present tense.

a The game _____ at 2:30 p.m., so let's get there early. (begin)

b We'd better hurry. The train _____ at 7:00 a.m. (leave)

c The train _____ in Milan at 6:24 p.m. (arrive)

d What time _____ the library _____ tomorrow? (open)

e When _____ the shops _____? (close)

3 Days, dates, and times

LANGUAGE FOCUS

Use prepositions with time expressions like this:

We could meet …	
on (+ day / date)	Friday July 10. the weekend.
in (+ month / year)	August. 2005.
at (+ time)	7 a.m. 2 p.m.
(no preposition)	this evening. tomorrow afternoon. next week.

You can combine time expressions like this:

We could meet …	(on)	Tuesday afternoon. Tuesday afternoon at 2 p.m.

Complete the sentences using *on*, *at*, *in*, or – (no preposition).

EXAMPLE   *Let's meet in the museum at 10:30 a.m.*

a   I'm really looking forward to your visit _____ November 5.

b   Should we meet _____ 6 o'clock?

c   The concert is _____ Friday.

d   I'll see you _____ tomorrow evening.

e   They are arriving in Japan _____ April.

4 Inviting

LANGUAGE FOCUS

You can write an invitation like this:

Do you want …	to go	to a party Saturday evening?
Would you like …		
How about going		

Write three invitations using these ideas. Think of your own day and time. Use a different expression each time.

_____

_____

_____

_____

_____

_____

5 Writing task 1

Write an invitation email to a foreign friend who is staying in your town or city. Use Alison's email in exercise 1.1 to help you.

6 Replying to an invitation

Complete the replies to Alison's invitation using these sentences. In Reply A Marta accepts the invitation. In Reply B she declines the invitation.

Can I bring some wine?
Sorry, but I can't make it.
Yes, I'd love to go to the party.
I'm going on a school trip to Boston this weekend.

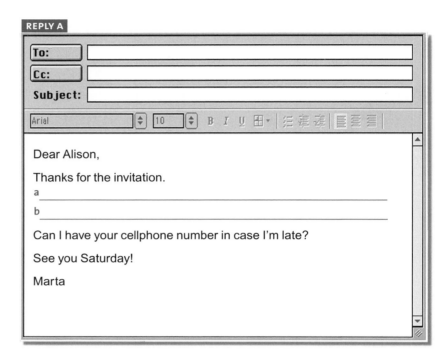

REPLY A

To:
Cc:
Subject:

Arial | 10 | B I U

Dear Alison,

Thanks for the invitation.

a _____

b _____

Can I have your cellphone number in case I'm late?

See you Saturday!

Marta

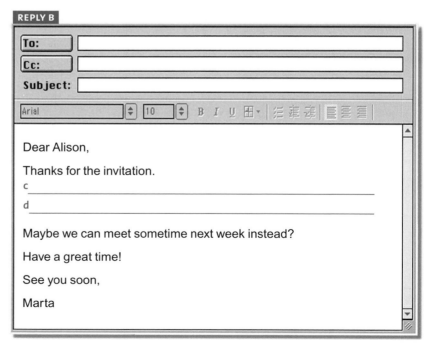

REPLY B

To:
Cc:
Subject:

Arial | 10 | B I U

Dear Alison,

Thanks for the invitation.

c _____

d _____

Maybe we can meet sometime next week instead?

Have a great time!

See you soon,

Marta

7 Replying to invitations

To ACCEPT an invitation:			To REFUSE an invitation:	
I'd love to		(have dinner).	I'd love to, but	I can't (make it).
Dinner	sounds	great.	I'm afraid	I'm busy.
That		like fun.	I'm sorry, but	

Write replies to these invitations.

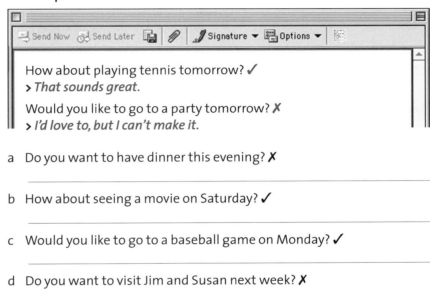

How about playing tennis tomorrow? ✓
> *That sounds great.*

Would you like to go to a party tomorrow? ✗
> *I'd love to, but I can't make it.*

a Do you want to have dinner this evening? ✗

b How about seeing a movie on Saturday? ✓

c Would you like to go to a baseball game on Monday? ✓

d Do you want to visit Jim and Susan next week? ✗

8 Suggesting another time to meet

If you refuse an invitation, you can suggest another time to meet:

Maybe we can meet	Saturday	
Why don't we meet	sometime next week	(instead)?
How about going	another time	

Rewrite these sentences in the correct order.

a instead? / we / don't / go / next / Why / week

b exhibition? / about / going / How / to / an

c free / Tuesday / Are / afternoon? / you

9 Writing task 2

Exchange your invitation email from exercise 5.1 with a partner. Write a reply, accepting or refusing the invitation. Use Marta's emails in exercise 6.1 to help you.

8 Making and changing arrangements

IN THIS UNIT, YOU WILL LEARN HOW TO...

▶ make a reservation

▶ write formal and informal emails about a change in plans

▶ write formal and informal apologies

1 An Internet advertisement

1 Jessica Davis is an American student. She wants to visit the Grand Canyon during spring break with a Japanese friend, Mari. She found this information on the Internet.

OLD OAK INN
Bed and Breakfast

900 Oak Avenue
Flagstaff
Arizona 75000

Telephone
(888) 850-1071
Fax
(888) 850-1072
Email
info@oldoakinn.com

Innkeeper
Donna Eastman

Rates
Twin rooms from $79.
Reservations
Advance reservations recommended.
Reservations guaranteed with Visa or Mastercard.
Cancelations
Full refund, minus $25 handling fee.

Check-in 4–6 p.m.,
Check-out 11 a.m.
No smoking. No pets.

Location
In Flagstaff, near downtown.

2 Complete these sentences about the Bed and Breakfast.

a Guests cannot bring their _____ to the Old Oak Inn.

b It's a good idea to make an advance _____ .

c There is a $25 _____ fee.

d You have to check out by _____ .

e The cheapest rooms cost _____ .

f The Old Oak Inn is near _____ Flagstaff.

2 Asking about accommodation

Read Jessica's email to the innkeeper quickly. What does she want to reserve?

a   breakfast for two people
b   a twin room for two nights
c   a single room for two people

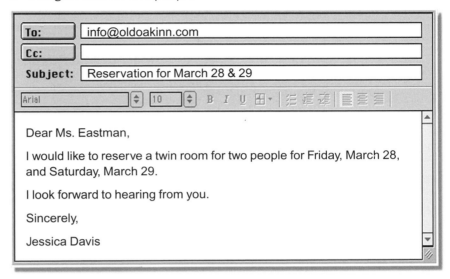

To: info@oldoakinn.com

Cc:

Subject: Reservation for March 28 & 29

Arial 10 B I U

Dear Ms. Eastman,

I would like to reserve a twin room for two people for Friday, March 28, and Saturday, March 29.

I look forward to hearing from you.

Sincerely,

Jessica Davis

3 Writing task 1

You and your friend want to visit Yellowstone National Park. Write a similar email to Craig Kelley at the Bed and Breakfast below. You want to reserve a twin room for (you choose days and dates).

THE OLD CREEK Bed and Breakfast

**3859 Miles Road
Dobson Creek
Wyoming 63000**

Telephone: (307) 225-1235; (800)420-8879
Fax: (307) 226-3677
http://www.oldcreek.com
Email: ckcreek@aol.com
Craig Kelley, Innkeeper.

Rates	Single rooms from $80, twin rooms from $95.
Reservations	Reservations guaranteed by major credit cards.
Cancelations	Full refund, minus $20 handling fee.
Location	10 minutes from Jackson Hole.
	Check-in 5–7 p.m., Check-out 11 a.m. No smoking. No children under 12.

4 Confirming a reservation

Read the correspondence between Ms. Eastman and Jessica. Underline the words or phrases in the emails which have a similar meaning to the following:

a I'm happy to tell you
b the cost of
c answer
d make sure of
e quick
f information
g at once
h room with two beds

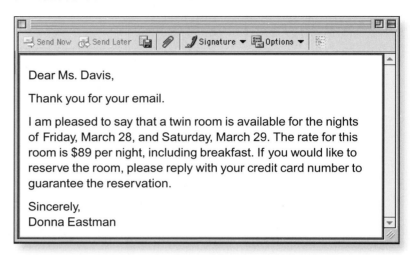

Dear Ms. Davis,

Thank you for your email.

I am pleased to say that a twin room is available for the nights of Friday, March 28, and Saturday, March 29. The rate for this room is $89 per night, including breakfast. If you would like to reserve the room, please reply with your credit card number to guarantee the reservation.

Sincerely,
Donna Eastman

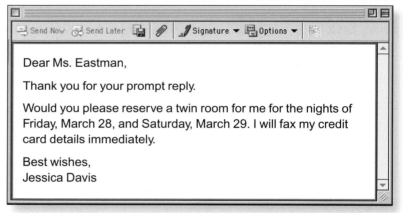

Dear Ms. Eastman,

Thank you for your prompt reply.

Would you please reserve a twin room for me for the nights of Friday, March 28, and Saturday, March 29. I will fax my credit card details immediately.

Best wishes,
Jessica Davis

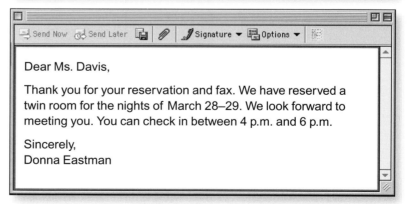

Dear Ms. Davis,

Thank you for your reservation and fax. We have reserved a twin room for the nights of March 28–29. We look forward to meeting you. You can check in between 4 p.m. and 6 p.m.

Sincerely,
Donna Eastman

5 Writing task 2

You received an email from Craig Kelley of the Old Creek, telling you that the room you requested is available. The rate is $95. Write a reply confirming your reservation. Use Jessica's email to help you.

6 Changing arrangements (informal)

1 Jessica received this email from Mari one week before their trip.

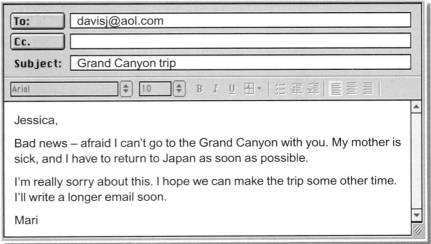

To:	davisj@aol.com
Cc.	
Subject:	Grand Canyon trip

Arial   10   B I U ⊞▾ | ⌸ ⌷ ⌸ | ⌸ ⌸ ⌸

Jessica,

Bad news – afraid I can't go to the Grand Canyon with you. My mother is sick, and I have to return to Japan as soon as possible.

I'm really sorry about this. I hope we can make the trip some other time. I'll write a longer email soon.

Mari

2 You can make an informal apology like this:

USEFUL LANGUAGE

(I'm) sorry, but (I'm) afraid	I can't	go to the movies meet you (for dinner)	tomorrow. on Sunday.

Write apologies to a friend for the situations below.

a meet / the park / this weekend

_____

_____

b go to the beach / Saturday morning

_____

_____

c meet / lunch tomorrow

_____

_____

d go ... (your idea – you choose where and when)

_____

_____

7 Giving a reason

1 When you write to someone you know to change plans, you should usually give a clear reason.

EXAMPLES

I have to go to the dentist.
My parents are visiting this weekend.
I have to study for my French test.

You can add the reason to your apology like this:
I'm sorry, but I can't join you Friday. I have to go to the dentist.

2 Write reasons for your apologies in exercise 6.2. You can use the ideas below or your own ideas.

b _____

c _____

d _____

8 Changing arrangements (formal)

1 Read the emails quickly.

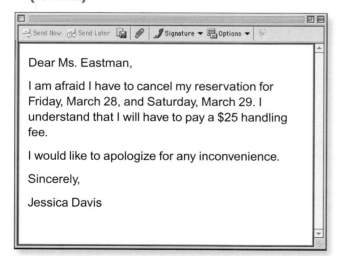

Dear Ms. Eastman,

I am afraid I have to cancel my reservation for Friday, March 28, and Saturday, March 29. I understand that I will have to pay a $25 handling fee.

I would like to apologize for any inconvenience.

Sincerely,

Jessica Davis

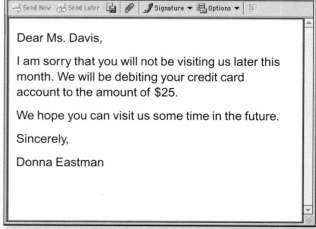

Dear Ms. Davis,

I am sorry that you will not be visiting us later this month. We will be debiting your credit card account to the amount of $25.

We hope you can visit us some time in the future.

Sincerely,

Donna Eastman

2   Now answer the questions.

    a Why is Jessica writing to Ms. Eastman?
    b Does she give a reason?
    c How much does she have to pay?
    d Does she apologize?
    e Do you think Ms. Eastman's reply is polite?

3   **LANGUAGE FOCUS**

When you write formally to someone about a change in arrangements:

    a use a polite tone
    b give specific details (date, time, reservation number)
    c keep your message brief
    d sign off with an apology

Note: You do not usually have to give a reason in business correspondence, but this will depend on the situation.

LANGUAGE FOCUS

To apologize politely, you can use these forms:

I am sorry, but	I have to cancel my reservation.
I am afraid	I am unable to attend the meeting on Sunday.
I regret to say	

I would like to apologize for	any inconvenience.
I hope this will not cause	
Please accept my apologies for	

Write apologies for the cancelations below. Use a different expression each time.

EXAMPLE your hotel reservation for January 29
I am sorry, but I have to cancel my hotel reservation for January 29.
I would like to apologize for any inconvenience.

    a your meeting for January 6 at 2 p.m.

    b your conference booking for July 10, reference IT063X

    c your appointment for 10:30 a.m. next Thursday

    d your reservation for a tennis court from 3:30 to 5:30 on Saturday

9 Writing task 3 Write to Craig Kelley, canceling your reservation. Use Jessica's email on the previous page to help you. You are writing three days before your scheduled arrival date.

9 Giving instructions

IN THIS UNIT, YOU WILL LEARN HOW TO ...

▶ give directions

▶ fax a map and cover sheet

▶ connect sentences using sequencing words (*then, and, when*)

1 An email from a friend

1 In-Sook is going to stay with a friend in London, and she receives an email giving directions to her friend's apartment.

> Dear In-Sook,
>
> I expect it's really hot in Korea right now. It's cool and sunny here at the moment. Just right for tennis.
>
> I'm afraid I can't meet you at the airport because I have some important meetings on Friday. But don't worry — my place is pretty easy to find.
>
> Here are the directions. I'll fax you a map of my local area later.
>
> From Heathrow Airport, take the London Underground Piccadilly Line to Leicester Square station and change to the Northern Line. Get out at Belsize Park station. The trip takes about an hour.
>
> When you leave Belsize Park station, turn left and go straight along the road. Park Hill Road is the third street on the left. Turn into Park Hill Road, then walk for about one minute. My flat is on the right — number 10. Just ring the bell! My flatmate Bridget will be there.
>
> See you Friday. Have a safe trip!
>
> Felicity

2 Are these statements true (T) or false (F)? Check (✓) the correct box.

		T	F
a	In-Sook is in England now.	☐	☐
b	In-Sook is going to visit Felicity on Friday.	☐	☐
c	Felicity is going to meet In-Sook at the airport.	☐	☐
d	In-Sook has to change trains.	☐	☐
e	Felicity's house is near Belsize Park station.	☐	☐

3 Look at the map of the London Underground and mark In-Sook's route.

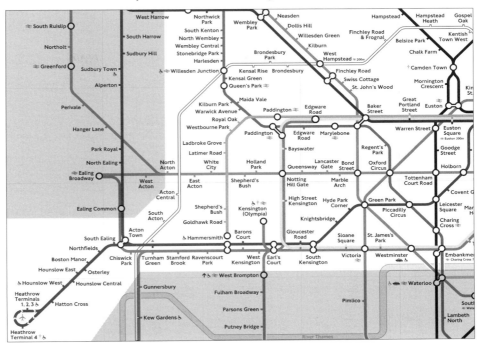

2 Sending a fax message

TIP!

mobile	= cellphone
local area	= neighborhood
flatmate	= roommate
flat	= apartment
underground	= subway
railway station	= train station

1 When you send an informal fax message, you can use a cover sheet including the following information:

— the name of the person the message is for
— the date
— your name
— your fax and phone numbers (+ your cellphone number and email address if appropriate)
— total number of pages
— a short message.

2 Write the details of Felicity's fax in the correct places below.

In-Sook Park   2 (including this one)   Felicity Webster
0208-341-1816   August 29, 2004

Date:	a _____
To:	b _____
From:	c _____
Phone:	d _____
Fax:	*0208–341–1874*
Pages:	e _____

▶ See pages 111–12 for more information about faxes.

3 Felicity wrote In-Sook a message on her fax cover sheet. Which message do you think Felicity wrote? Check (✓) the box.

> Dear In-Sook,
> a Could you send me a map of your local area, please? ☐
> b Here are the directions from the airport to
>   Leicester Square. ☐
> c Here's the map! ☐
> d What's the weather like in Korea? ☐
>   Bye!
>   Felicity

4 This is Felicity's map of her local area. Mark the route from Belsize Park station, and circle Felicity's flat.

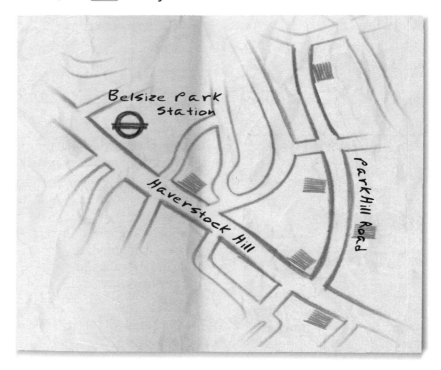

3 Giving directions

1 You can use these directions to help people use public transport:

USEFUL LANGUAGE		
Take		the Central line to Oxford Circus. the Brighton train from Victoria station.
		any bus from stop number 3. the number 6 bus outside the station.
Get out	at	the last stop. Euston station.
It The trip		takes 30 minutes. costs £5.00.

Complete the directions to In-Sook's university in Busan.

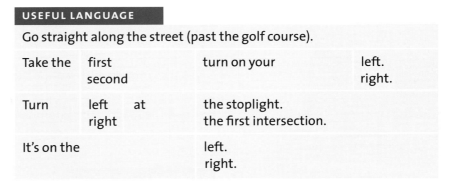

a _____ the Line 1 subway from Busan Yok Station, and
b _____ out at Somyon station. Then take c_____
number 8 bus outside the station. Get out d_____ the Dong-
Eui University stop. You can walk up the hill or take a shuttle bus. The
whole trip e_____ about 1500 won.

2 You can use these directions for people walking, cycling, or driving:

Go straight along the street (past the golf course).

Take the	first		turn on your	left.
	second			right.
Turn	left	at	the stoplight.	
	right		the first intersection.	
It's on the			left.	
			right.	

Write directions to each place on the map.

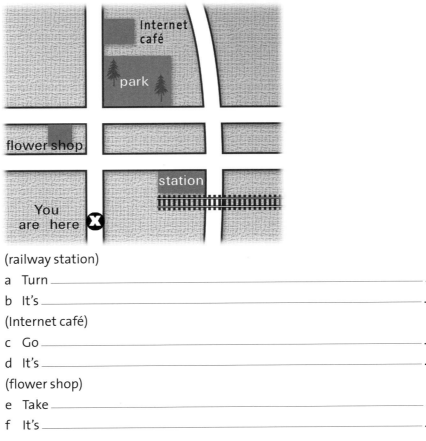

(railway station)

a Turn _____ .

b It's _____ .

(Internet café)

c Go _____ .

d It's _____ .

(flower shop)

e Take _____ .

f It's _____ .

4 Sequencing words

TIP!

and and *then* have a similar meaning in these sentences.

1

LANGUAGE FOCUS

When you write directions, you can connect sentences with *and* like this:

Take the Piccadilly Line to Green Park station. Change to the Victoria Line.

Take the Piccadilly Line to Green Park station and change to the Victoria Line. (**Note**: don't use a comma before *and*.)

Take the Piccadilly Line to Green Park station, then change to the Victoria Line. (**Note**: use a comma before *then*.)

Connect the sentences below with *and* or *then*.

a   Go to the bus stop. Take any bus to King's Cross station.

_____

b   Take the District Line to Westminster station. Change to the Jubilee Line.

_____

c   Go to Hammersmith station. Go out of the east exit.

_____

d   Cross the road. Catch a number 6 bus.

_____

2

LANGUAGE FOCUS

You can connect two sentences with *when* like this:

Leave Belsize Park station. Turn left.
When you leave Belsize Park station, turn left.

Connect the phrases below with *when*.

a   reach the bank / turn right

_____

b   see the post office / wait outside

_____

c   get to the traffic light / go straight

_____

d   get off the bus / cross the road

_____

3   Complete the sentences, using *and*, *then*, or *when*. Pay attention to punctuation.

a   _____ you reach the bank, turn left.

b   Go to Green Park station, _____ take the Victoria line.

c   Go to the bus stop _____ take a number 4 bus.

d   _____ you leave the building, turn right.

e   Take the Central Line to Bond Street station _____ change to the Jubilee line.

f   Go to the end of the street, _____ turn right.

5 Writing task 1

You are studying in Montreal and living in an apartment near Saint-Michel subway station. A friend is going to visit you. Write directions from Montreal University. Use Felicity's email to help you.

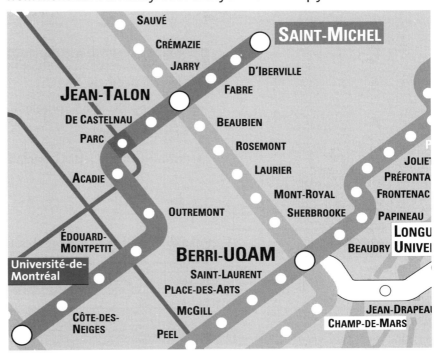

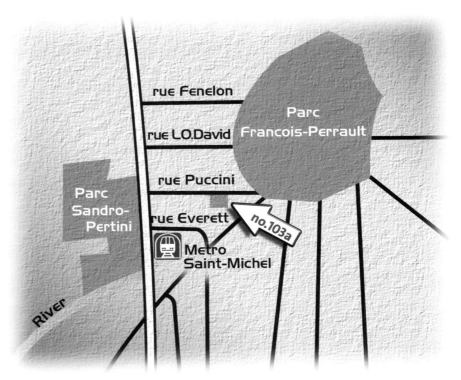

6 Writing task 2

A foreign friend is going to visit your house or apartment. Email him or her directions from the town / city center. Prepare a map and fax it with a cover sheet.

10 Dealing with problems

IN THIS UNIT, YOU WILL LEARN HOW TO ...

▶ complain politely

▶ describe a situation / problem

▶ suggest a solution

▶ write an email / letter complaining about a service or product

1 A complaint

1 Read the email to an Internet bookseller quickly. Why is Ricardo writing?

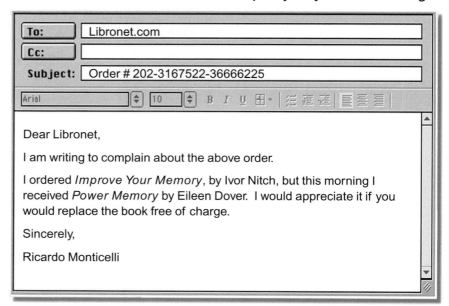

To: Libronet.com

Cc:

Subject: Order # 202-3167522-36666225

Arial   10   B I U 田▾ ⋮≡ ≡ ⋮ ≣ ≣ ≣

Dear Libronet,

I am writing to complain about the above order.

I ordered *Improve Your Memory*, by Ivor Nitch, but this morning I received *Power Memory* by Eileen Dover. I would appreciate it if you would replace the book free of charge.

Sincerely,

Ricardo Monticelli

2 Now answer the questions.
a What did Ricardo order?
b What is the problem?
c What does he want Libronet to do?
d Does he want to pay Libronet more money?

2 Writing a complaint

Fill in the blanks, using the words below.

explain   possible   reference   polite   solving

When you write a complaint letter, fax, or email, you should …

a   include a _____ number, if you have one.

b   send the complaint as soon as _____.

c   _____ the situation clearly.

d   suggest a way of _____ the problem.

e   be _____.

3 Reference numbers

1   **If you have a reference number, you should write it at the beginning of your complaint.**

In an email, you can use the subject line:

To:	Drums and Drummer Magazine<drumsanddrummer.com>
Cc:	
Subject:	Subscription VS 332189

Arial   10   B I U

I wrote to you on September 20 regarding my subscription …

In a letter or fax, you can write the number as a separate, underlined first line:

Dear Mr. Glazunov,

RE: ACCOUNT # 076631K
I am writing about the above account …

You can also write the number in the main text:

Dear Penzance,

I am writing with reference to my latest order (X23-00011-32)
for six garden chairs. They arrived yesterday, but …

2 Look at these two letters. complete the letters with these phrases.

Mr. Stevens   my account (#773206)   regarding my order   RF553

Dear Sir/Madam,

Re: order ^a_____

I am writing ^b_____ for six widescreen television sets. I ordered them three weeks ago, but they have not arrived. Please let me know when to expect delivery.

Sincerely yours,

James Cameron

Dear ^c_____

I am writing about ^d_____

I would appreciate it if you would send me a statement for this month.

Regards,

Mary Stewart

4 Complaining

Don't use emotional language, e.g. *disgusted*, or words like *fault* or *blame*.

You can use these expressions to begin your message:

USEFUL LANGUAGE

I am writing	to complain about …
	about a problem with …
	with reference to …
	about …

The first two expressions have a stronger complaining tone.

Write sentences to complain. Use a different expression each time.

a order # 7214-649 (Conex digital camera)
   I am writing to complain about order # 7214-649 (Conex digital camera).

b my subscription to your magazine

   _____

   _____

c the meal I ate at your restaurant on October 27

   _____

   _____

d item #346-2001 (skirt)

   _____

   _____

5 Explaining the situation

1

When you make a complaint, you can combine contrasting information like this:

The chairs arrived yesterday. (fact)
They were damaged. (complaint)

The chairs arrived yesterday, but they were damaged.

Match the sentences (a–d) with the complaints (1–4). Then connect the sentences with *but*.

a I ordered a small skirt.
b I ordered the camera three weeks ago.
c I reserved a table by the window.
d I received the August and October issues.

1 I am still waiting for delivery.
2 It was next to the kitchen.
3 I received a large one.
4 I did not receive the September issue.

I ordered a small skirt, but _____

_____

_____

_____

_____

_____

_____

2 Write a similar sentence using one of the situations below or your own idea.

_____

_____

6 Requesting action

1 When you want someone to do something, you can use these expressions:

USEFUL LANGUAGE		
Please	send a replacement	as soon as possible.
I would appreciate it if you would	give me a refund	
	replace (the jeans) free of charge.	

Write similar sentences using the following ideas.

a send me the correct size
Please send me the correct size.

b refund the price of the meal

_____

c send me the missing issue

_____

d confirm that you shipped the order

_____

2 Write the sentences from exercise 5.1. Then write the matching sentences from exercise 6.1.

a *I ordered a small skirt, but I received a large one. Please send me the correct size.*

b _____

c _____

d _____

7 Polite or impolite?

Which sentence in each pair is NOT polite? Mark it with a cross (X).

a I'm not satisfied with your product. ☐ Your product is garbage. ☐

b Send me a refund immediately! ☐ I would like a refund. ☐

c I am disgusted with your service. ☐ I am unhappy with your service. ☐

d The printer doesn't work. ☐ The stupid printer is useless. ☐

e You are completely dishonest. ☐ I think you overcharged me. ☐

f The bathroom wasn't clean. ☐ Do you ever clean the bathrooms? ☐

8 Writing task 1 **1** Choose one of the situations below. Then write a complaint email, letter, or fax.

> Company: Hard Wear (clothes manufacturers)
> Situation: You ordered a pair of jeans last week. The order number is ku604-203.
> Problem: The jeans arrived this morning. They are the wrong color. They are blue – you ordered black.
> Solution: You want the company to change the jeans.

> Company: Peppy Pizza (pizza delivery service chain)
> Situation: You ordered two pizzas from your local Peppy Pizza branch last night.
> Problem: The pizzas made you and your friend sick.
> Solution: You want your money refunded.

2 Find a partner who chose the same situation, and compare your work.

9 Writing task 2 Work with a partner. Write a complaint explaining the situation and requesting action. Use one of the situations from exercise 5.2 or your own idea. Before you start, make notes below.

Company name

Problem

Reference number

Solution

Review 2

1 Making reservations

1 Read this fax from Melissa. Why is she writing? Check (✓) the correct answer.

a She is going to fax a map. ☐
b She is paying for her hotel room. ☐
c She wants to make a reservation. ☐

To	Cosmopolitan Hotel	Subject	Reservation
From	Melissa Cox	No. of pages	1
Date	June 1, 2005		

Dear Cosmopolitan Hotel,

Thank you for your email. I am writing to ᵃ_____ my reservation for 2 people for 3 nights, July 24, 25, and 26. I would like to pay with my VISA ᵇ_____. Here is the number: 4399 2948 381 2833. The expiration ᶜ_____ is March 2010. The ᵈ_____ is $125.00 per night, so please charge my card for $375.00.

I look ᵉ_____ to seeing you on July 24. Can you tell me how to get from the bus station to the hotel? Thank you for all your ᶠ_____ .

Sincerely,
Melissa Cox

2 Now complete the fax with these words:

help   forward   date   confirm   card   rate

3 Read the Cosmopolitan Hotel's answer to Melissa. There are three mistakes in the fax (punctuation, capitalization, and spelling). (Circle) each mistake.

Dear Ms. Cox,

Thank you for sending your credit card infomation. We have charged your card for $475.00 as you asked.

We look forward to seeing you on june 24. Check-in time is, from 3:00–8:00 p.m.

Best wishes,
The Cosmopolitan Hotel

P.S. We are faxing a map with directions from the bus station to the hotel.

4 Now correct the Cosmopolitan Hotel's mistakes. Write the complete corrected sentences below.

a _____

b _____

c _____

5 After Melissa received the fax from the hotel, she sent an email. Complete her paragraphs by writing the missing sentences from the list below.

a Please refund $100 to my credit card.
b Could you send me a fax confirming this information?
c I am writing to complain about the fax I received.
d Please accept my apologies for any inconvenience.

To:	Cosmopolitan Hotel
Cc:	
Subject:	Reservation #200187

Arial · 10 · B I U ⊞▾ ⋮≣ ≣ ≣ ≣ ≣ ≣

Dear Cosmopolitan Hotel,

1 _____ You said that you were charging me $475 for three nights, but the charge should be $375 for three nights (3 x $125 per night = $375).
2 _____ In addition, you said that you would see me on June 24. But my friend and I are coming on July 24.

I know that check-in is from 3:00-8:00, but unfortunately we will not be able to check in until after 9:00 pm on July 24, because our plane arrives at 7:45 p.m.
3 _____
4 _____ Thank you for the map.

Sincerely,
Melissa Cox

---

2 Directions

Look at the map of an area of London. Then write instructions from the underground exit to your flat.

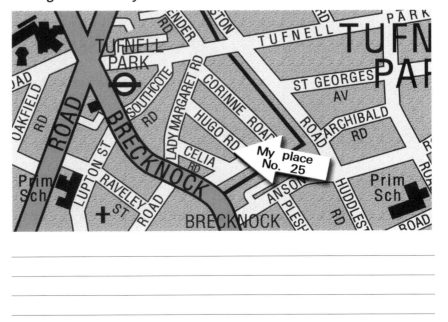

_____

_____

_____

_____

3 Complaints and solutions

Read the complaints below. Then write the appropriate solution.

1 The book I received was used, not new.

_____

  a Please discount the price.
  b Could you send me a magazine instead?

2 I have been waiting for my CDs for four weeks.

_____

  c Please send my order as soon as possible.
  d Please replace the CDs free of charge.

3 The price on the Internet for a room was $79.00, but you charged my credit card $129.00.

_____

  e Please let me have a second room.
  f Please send me a refund.

4 The software I ordered doesn't work on my computer.

_____

  g Please send me a free computer.
  h Can I exchange the software for another version?

5 I ordered a medium, but I received a large.

_____

  i Please send me a replacement.
  j How much should I pay for a large?

4 Pairwork dictation

1 Work with a partner. Take turns reading sentences to your partner, who will write them down. Student A, use the sentences on page 105. Student B, use the sentences on page 106.

> **USEFUL LANGUAGE**
>
> Could you say that again?
> Could you speak more slowly?
> How do you spell "…"?
> What's the (fourth) word?

Now, write the sentences that your partner reads.

a _____

b _____

c _____

d _____

e _____

f _____

2 When you are finished, compare your sentences with your partner's page. Did you write everything correctly?

5 Word puzzle

Write the answers to the clues below in the puzzle. When you are finished, read down to find the answer to this question:

What do you have to do with a reservation if you can't come as planned?

a If your product is damaged, you should write to c_____ .

b "Take c_____" is a common informal close.

c Walk for about 5 m_____ .

d A ticket c_____ $3.45.

e Don't f_____ to bring an umbrella!

f We c_____ meet on Saturday at 10:00.

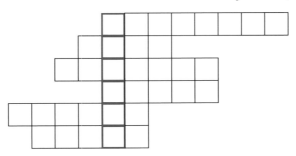

6 Writing and culture: greeting cards

1 In your country, when do people send and receive cards? Make a list, and then share it with a partner or small group.

TIP!

English speakers like to send paper or electronic greeting cards for holidays and special occasions.

2 Write the messages below in the correct order. Then complete the appropriate card.

1 merry Christmas / and a happy / Have a / New Year

2 wedding / Congratulations / your / on

3 wishes / Very / birthday / your / for / best

4 Valentine's / Happy / Day

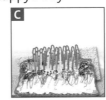

LANGUAGE FOCUS

You can use language like this for special occasions:

Congratulations on	your new job. your engagement. passing your exams!
Have a happy	Halloween. anniversary.

With a partner, design a greeting card. Choose an occasion, and write a message. Don't forget to draw a picture! Show your card to another pair.

11 Describing

▶ describe a place (campus, neighborhood)

▶ describe a room, apartment, or house

▶ describe a person

1 An email to a friend

1 Read the email.

To: Yun Min

Cc:

Subject: Hello from the University of Oregon!

Arial | 10 | B I U ⊞ ▾ | ⋮≡ ⫶≡ ⫶≡ | ≣ ≣ ≣

Dear Yun Min,

Well, I started the English course on Monday. I was nervous, but excited, too.

The university campus is really big. There are a few shops on campus, and some great cafés nearby.

I'm staying with a nice family near the campus. My room gets plenty of sun, which is nice. The neighborhood is quiet, and there's a big park with a lot of big trees.

My classmates are great, and I often hang out with Carlos and Maria from Venezuela. They're very friendly, and they speak good English, too.

I'll only be here for one month, but I hope I'll learn a lot of English.

Write soon,

Susumu

---

2 Are these statements true (T) or false (F)? Check (✓) the correct box.

		T	F
a	Susumu is studying English at the University of Oregon.	☐	☐
b	The campus is big and has a lot of shops.	☐	☐
c	He is staying with a family near downtown.	☐	☐
d	He doesn't like his room.	☐	☐
e	He has some Venezuelan classmates.	☐	☐

1

Look at these pairs of adjectives:

If something is *exciting*,	you feel *excited*.
boring	*bored*
interesting	*interested*
frightening	*frightened*
annoying	*annoyed*
tiring	*tired*

Fill in the blanks using *ing* adjectives from the *Language focus* box.

a   My hometown is pretty _____ . Nothing ever happens there.

b   Running is more _____ than swimming. I usually swim for an hour, but I can only run for thirty minutes.

c   Kurt can be very _____ . He often borrows my things without asking.

d   I am reading a good book about genetics. It's _____ .

e   Our plane made an emergency landing. It was really _____ .

f   The game was really _____ . My team scored in the final minute!

2   **Fill in the blanks using *ed* adjectives from the *Language focus* box.**

a   It's my birthday tomorrow. I'm really _____ !

b   I felt _____ after playing baseball, so I went straight home.

c   Julia is _____ with her boyfriend. They had a fight last tonight.

d   I always feel _____ if I stay at home. I prefer to go out and have fun.

e   Kok-Wing is _____ in yoga.

f   We crossed the river on a rope bridge. I was a little _____ , to be honest!

3 Describing your neighborhood

1

Look at these sentences. You can connect them like this:

There's a park. It has a lot of trees.
There's a park with a lot of trees.

Connect these sentences with *with*.

a   There's a museum. It has some interesting exhibits.

_____

b   There's a library. It has free Internet access.

_____

c   There's a mall. It has a lot of stores.

_____

d   There's a pond. It has ducks and geese.

_____

2   Correct the mistakes in this description, then rewrite it. There are six mistakes, including two missing words.

My new neighborhood is OK, but it's not very interested. There are a lot private houses and apartment building, and there is a small park with a pond. Near the station, there are a nice coffee shop. I sometimes meet my friends there. There's also new movie theater, but it always has bored movies!

3   Write a similar paragraph about your neighborhood (without the mistakes!).

_____

_____

_____

_____

_____

4 Describing where you live

1   You can describe where you live like this:

I live	in a	small large medium-sized	room. apartment. house.
	alone.		
	with	my parents. a friend. my sister.	
I share	the apartment	with	a friend. my sister.

You can connect two sentences like this:

My room is sunny. This is nice.

My room is sunny, which is nice.

Here *this* and *which* both mean "the fact that the room is sunny".

Connect the sentences below with *which*.

a My parents' house is near the station. This is convenient.

_____

b I share an apartment with friends. This is fun.

_____

c There's a small store across the street. This is useful.

_____

d I live in a small room. This is uncomfortable.

_____

2 **Look at the picture and the description. Circle the correct information,**

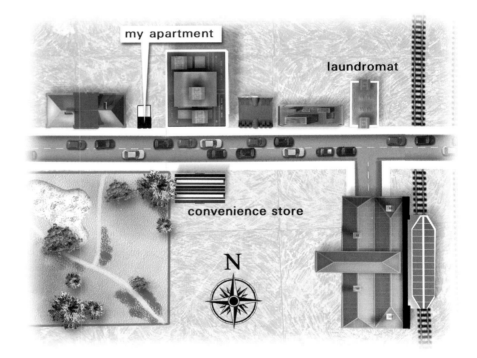

I live alone in a small apartment. It's a (a) *five-minute / thirty-minute* walk from the station. There's a (b) *laundromat / convenience store* across the street, which comes in handy. The apartment is (c) *sunny / dark*, but it's (d) *on / near* a busy road, so it's noisy. It's also (e) *next to / across from* the park. I go jogging there most mornings.

3 **Write a similar paragraph about your room or apartment.**

5 Describing a person

1 Match the sentences on the left with the ones on the right.

a   Amy is a hard-working student.
b   Ms. Wang is very patient.
c   Andy is a really interesting guy.
d   Tessa is smart.
e   Heinz is always cheerful.
f   Prof. Aziz is very friendly.
g   Jenny is really generous.

1   She can use all sorts of computer software.
2   He knows a lot about so many things.
3   She studies late every evening.
4   He's always smiling and joking.
5   She loves making cakes and cookies for her friends.
6   She never loses her temper.
7   He often chats with students outside class.

2 The adjectives in exercise 1 (sentences a–g) have a positive meaning. The adjectives below have a negative meaning. Match the positive adjectives with their negative opposites below.

| unfriendly | impatient | boring | bad-tempered |
| lazy | stingy | unintelligent | |

positive	negative
hard-working	lazy

3 Work with a partner. Write some more positive words to describe people. If you can, write their opposites, too.

6 Abilities and interests

1 You can describe abilities and interests like this:

Ken	can	play the guitar. speak French.	
	is	good at	English. swimming.
	is interested in likes	old cars. skateboarding.	
		skiing. taking photographs.	

Speak to four different classmates. Ask each one a different question below, and take notes.

	name	notes
EXAMPLE What can do?	Junko	ride a motorbike
What can you do?		
What are you good at?		
What are you interested in?		
What do you like doing?		

2   **Write a complete sentence about each classmate.**

EXAMPLE   *Junko can ride a motorbike.*

_____

_____

_____

_____

7 Writing task

Choose one of these tasks.

a   Think about your first days at college or university. Write an email to a friend. You can use Susumu's email on page 70 to help you.

b   You have just started a short summer course in a foreign country. Write an email to a friend in your own country or another country. You can use Susumu's email on page 70 to help you.

12 Giving an opinion and recommending

IN THIS UNIT, YOU WILL LEARN HOW TO ...

► write your opinion of a store / restaurant / club

► describe it, and recommend its services

► write about recent experiences using the present perfect and simple past

► write about locations

1 Some emails

1 Read the emails quickly. Which email is about ...

a   an Internet café? ☐
b   a CD store? ☐
c   a university movie club? ☐

1 Have you been to Netcafé? It's across from the bank. It has really fast computers, and you can stay as long as you want. I recommend it. The choice of drinks is good, too.

2 Have you heard about the movie club? I joined last week and saw *The Ring*. We watch all kinds of movies, and there's always a discussion afterwards. We meet in room 203 every Friday evening. Why don't you try it?

3 Have you checked out Dr. Jazz? It's a CD store across from McDonald's. I went there this morning, and found some Miles Davis CDs. It specializes in jazz and blues. It's certainly worth a visit!

2 Are these statements true (T) or false (F)? Check (✓) the correct box.

	T	F
a Netcafé is next to the bank.	☐	☐
b There isn't a good selection of drinks at Netcafé.	☐	☐
c The movie club meets once a week.	☐	☐
d Dr. Jazz is above McDonald's.	☐	☐
e It specializes in jazz and hip-hop.	☐	☐

2 Asking about recent experiences

LANGUAGE FOCUS

You can use the present perfect tense to ask about recent experiences with or without the time expression *yet*:

Have you tried Pierre's restaurant (yet)?

Write questions about these places.

a go to the multiplex

_____

b check out the new bookstore

_____

c see the new karaoke bar

_____

d try the Mocha coffee shop

_____

3 Location

TIP!

In the U.S. the floor at street level is called the *first floor*. In Europe it is the *ground floor*, and the floor above it is the *first floor*.

Write about the location of each place on the map.

USEFUL LANGUAGE

It's	next to near across from	the bank. the park.
	on	the fifth floor. the top floor.
	above	the drugstore.

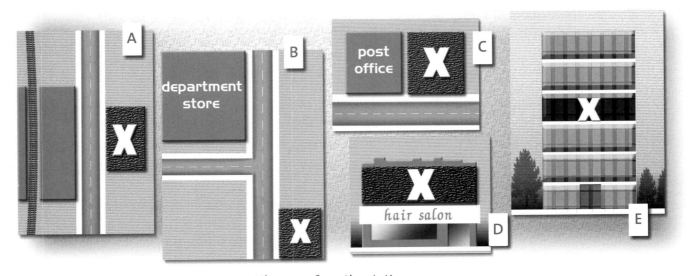

a It's *across from* the station.
b It's _____ the department store.
c It's _____ the post office.
d It's _____ the hair salon.
e It's _____ the 4th floor.

4 Past experiences

LANGUAGE FOCUS

To write about recent completed experiences with a time expression, use the simple past:
I went shopping with my friend last week.

Write the correct form of the verb in each sentence.

a I _____ lunch there yesterday. (have)

b Keiko and I _____ the art gallery on Wednesday. (visit)

c I _____ a free tennis lesson there last week. (take)

d I _____ the new James Bond movie there last night. (see)

e We _____ a couple of DVDs there last night. (rent)

5 Describing goods and services

1 Match the places (1–4) with the statements below (a–h).

1 restaurant   3 bookstore
2 jeans store   4 movie theater

a It has a good travel section. ☐   e The seats are comfortable. ☐
b The screen is very large. ☐   f It sells foreign magazines. ☐
c It has a lot of styles. ☐   g The waiters are rude. ☐
d The food is expensive. ☐   h It sells all the top brands. ☐

2 Write about each place. Connect the sentences above with *and*.

a restaurant
   The food is expensive, and the waiters are rude.

b jeans store

_____

c bookstore

_____

d movie theater

_____

6 Recommending

★★★★★	excellent	I highly recommend it.
★★★★	very good	I recommend it. Check it out.
★★★	average	OK, but nothing special.
★★	not very good	I don't recommend it. Give it a miss.
★	terrible	I don't recommend it at all!

Write a suitable comment for each place.

a restaurant ★★★★★
  It's excellent. I highly recommend it.

b movie theater ★★★★

_____

c CD store ★★

_____

d hair salon ★

_____

e department store ★★★

_____

f game center ★★★★★

_____

7 A new store

Read these notes about a new store, then write about it below. When you have finished, compare your recommendation with a partner.

- Sandwich Express -
new place - near the Central Hotel
- bought lunch - yesterday -
sells great sandwiches, salads, and sushi -
very good - check it out!

Have you heard about _____

_____

_____

_____

_____

8 On the Internet

1 Read these reviews for a movie, a CD, and a book. Write the correct heading (a–c) for each review.

a *Internet Made Easy*, by Suzie Ryman
b *The Power Ring*
c CD: *Björn's Greatest Hits*

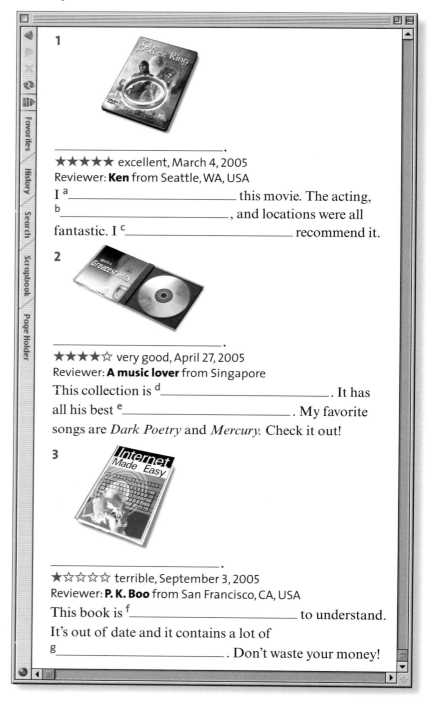

1

_____.
★★★★★ excellent, March 4, 2005
Reviewer: **Ken** from Seattle, WA, USA
I ᵃ_____ this movie. The acting,
ᵇ_____, and locations were all
fantastic. I ᶜ_____ recommend it.

2

_____.
★★★★☆ very good, April 27, 2005
Reviewer: **A music lover** from Singapore
This collection is ᵈ_____. It has
all his best ᵉ_____. My favorite
songs are *Dark Poetry* and *Mercury.* Check it out!

3

_____.
★☆☆☆☆ terrible, September 3, 2005
Reviewer: **P. K. Boo** from San Francisco, CA, USA
This book is ᶠ_____ to understand.
It's out of date and it contains a lot of
ᵍ_____. Don't waste your money!

2 Read the reviews again, and fill in the blanks. Use the words below.

errors	great	highly	tracks
loved	difficult	soundtrack	

9 Writing task

1 Write a short email to a friend recommending one of the things below. Use the emails in exercise 1.1 to help you.

coffee shop   website   nightclub   university club

2 Write a short review of a movie, CD, or book for an Internet store website. You can use the examples in exercise 8.1 to help you. Look at customers' reviews on real websites, too.

13 Writing about a vacation

> **IN THIS UNIT, YOU WILL LEARN HOW TO …**
>
> ▶ write about recent experiences
>
> ▶ describe places, people, and things

1 An email to a friend

1 Read the email.

To:	Jane Grand<janegrand@aol.com>
Cc:	
Subject:	Spain

Arial | 10 | B I U ⊞ ▾ | ⋮≡ ⋲≡ ⋱≡ | ≡ ≡ ≡

Dear Jane,

I got back home yesterday. Kimiko and I had a wonderful time in Spain. We did some sightseeing, ate some great food, and took a lot of photos.

We went to Seville, then Granada, and saw the Alhambra. It was fantastic – crowded, but very interesting. We spent the whole day there.

One other thing – while we were waiting to get into the Alhambra, we saw Tom Cruise! Well, I think it was him, anyway …

See you soon,

Hyun Sil

2 Are these statements true (T) or false (F)? Check (✓) the correct box.

		T	F
a	Hyun Sil has just returned from her vacation.	☐	☐
b	She enjoyed herself very much.	☐	☐
c	She and Kimiko visited Granada first.	☐	☐
d	There weren't many people in the Alhambra.	☐	☐
e	They spent only a short time there.	☐	☐
f	She thinks she saw Tom Cruise.	☐	☐

2 Did you have a good time?

You can talk about how you spent your time like this:

USEFUL LANGUAGE

I	had a	fantastic ☺☺	vacation
We Luigi and I		great	weekend
		good ☺	time (in the U.S).
	didn't have a very good ☹		
	had a terrible ☹☹		

Write a sentence about each picture below.

a _____

b _____

c _____

d _____

3 What did you do?

LANGUAGE FOCUS

Look at these sentences:
We did some sightseeing.
We ate some great food.
We took a lot of photos.

We can connect sentences like this:
We did some sightseeing, ate some great food,
and took a lot of photos.

Connect the activities below to make sentences using the simple past tense.

relax on the beach   make a lot of new friends
go to clubs every night

a We _____

_____

visit some temples   buy some great souvenirs
try to use my Japanese

b I _____

_____

take English classes every morning   go to a movie or a show in
visit museums in the afternoon   the evening

c I _____

_____

4 What was it like?   1

You can combine adjectives that are both positive or both negative with *and*:
The town was lively and interesting. (positive + positive)
The town was ugly and noisy.   (negative + negative)

You can combine a positive and a negative adjective with *but*:
The town was interesting but noisy. (positive + negative)
The town was small but lively.   (negative + positive)

Combine the adjectives with *and* or *but*:

a The weather was   hot _____ sunny.
                       mild _____ changeable.
                       cold _____ rainy.

b The hotel was   cheap _____ dirty.
                       cheap _____ clean.
                       expensive _____ noisy.

c The beach was   dirty _____ crowded.
                       beautiful _____ clean.
                       clean _____ crowded.

d The food was   cheap _____ delicious.
                       delicious _____ expensive.
                       disgusting _____ expensive.

2 Write the words below on the correct lines in the table.

wonderful   so-so   awful   all right
horrible   great   fantastic terrible

very good = _____

OK = _____

very bad = _____

3

Look at these sentences:

"Very good" adjective + two positive adjectives:
The nightlife was *fantastic* – *lively* and *interesting*.

"Very bad" adjective + two negative adjectives:
The town was *awful* – *ugly* and *noisy*.

"OK" adjective + one positive and one negative adjective:
The town was *so-so* – *pretty* but *noisy*.

Note that you can use a dash (–) to connect the two parts of a sentence.

Write one similar sentence for each of the following topics.

Weather _____

Hotel _____.

Beach _____

Food _____

4 Work with a partner. Write sentences about a vacation using your own ideas, or the pictures below.

_____

_____

_____

the beach   the hotel   the train

the food   the nightclub

5 What were you doing when it happened?

1

We often use the past continuous and simple past tense together when the shorter action interrupts the longer one:
We were waiting to get into the Alhambra.
We saw Tom Cruise.

You can combine the sentences like this:
While we were waiting to get into the Alhambra, we saw Tom Cruise.

Connect these sentences with *while*.

a We were dancing. The fire alarm sounded.

_____

_____

c We were swimming at the beach. There was a shark warning.

_____

_____

b I was taking some pictures. I dropped my camera.

_____

_____

d I was waiting in the airport lounge. I met an old school friend.

_____

_____

2 Write a similar sentence about youself. It can be true or imaginary.

_____

6 A disastrous vacation

1 Look at the pictures of Jack's vacation, and complete the postcard.

Dear Eri,

I'm writing this card at the airport. We had a ª _____ vacation! The weather was ᵇ_____ – it ᶜ _____ every day, and it was very ᵈ _____ . The mountains were beautiful, but I ᵉ _____ my traveler's checks, so we ᶠ _____ cup noodles every day. While we were ᵍ _____ , Dave ʰ _____ and ⁱ _____ his leg. It's great to be coming home!

See you soon,

Jack

New Zealand

2 Work with a partner, and compare your postcards.

7 Writing task

Think of a real trip or vacation you have been on, or use your imagination. You have just returned home. Write an email to a classmate telling him / her about it. Use the ideas below to help you.

Food   Weather   Hotel   Beaches
Tourist sites Shopping   Nightlife

14 Writing about an interest

IN THIS UNIT, YOU WILL LEARN HOW TO ...

▶ write about a personal interest for a personal home page

▶ arrange your ideas into paragraphs

▶ write captions for photographs

1 A home page

1 Read this section of a personal home page. Who is the writer writing for? Check (✓) one or more boxes.

a his / her friends and family ☐
b his / her college teacher ☐
c anybody who finds the home page ☐
d music professors ☐

a _____
Reggae is a type of popular music. It has a very strong rhythm, and many songs are about poverty, social injustice, and religion.

b _____
Reggae began in Jamaica in the late 1960s as the music of poor people. Some famous musicians were Peter Tosh and Jimmy Cliff, but the biggest star was Bob Marley.

c _____
I became a reggae fan when I was about 16. I found some of my parents' old records. Bob Marley was my favorite, and I learned all the words of his songs by heart.

d _____
I like listening to reggae, but I also love to play it. I started to learn the guitar a few years ago. Now I play in my own band – "The Moaners". We play original songs and covers of old classics, such as "I Shot the Sheriff."

Here are a few photos of our band.

1 One of our gigs   2 Me and my guitar

2 Complete the home page by writing these headings above the matching paragraphs.

How I became interested in reggae   My band
Introduction   History

2 Topic sentences

1

When we write in English, we use paragraphs to organize topics. The first sentence of a paragraph is usually the *topic sentence*. A topic sentence explains the subject of a paragraph.

Write the best topic sentence to complete the paragraph. Choose from the sentences (1–3) below.

a _____

They have long floppy ears, and long noses. They don't have long legs, though, so they can't run very fast. My dog is called Horace. We got him when he was a tiny puppy – only eight weeks old! Here's a picture of him! [Horace]

1   I take my dog for a walk every day.
2   Dogs can catch fleas in summer.
3   Basset hounds are my favorite type of dog.

b _____

I eat soybean products like tofu, instead. I eat lots of fruit and vegetables, too. For breakfast, I usually have fruit and yogurt. While I'm at college, I eat at the cafeteria, and often have pasta for lunch. In the evening, I eat with my friends. They think I'm crazy not to eat meat, but it's my choice!

1   I never eat potatoes or carrots.
2   I'm a vegetarian, so I don't eat meat.
3   I like cows and pigs.

2   **Read the text on the next page. It's part of a home page about photography. Write the topic sentences below at the beginning of the correct paragraphs.**

After I left school, I started developing my films at home.
I have been interested in photography since I was a kid.
I bought my first digital camera about two years ago.
I joined my school photography club when I was 12.
I just bought a new digital camera.

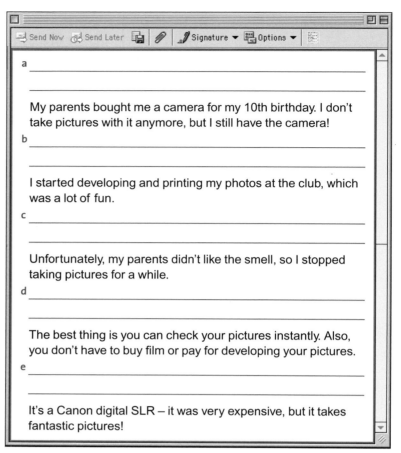

a _____
_____

My parents bought me a camera for my 10th birthday. I don't take pictures with it anymore, but I still have the camera!

b _____
_____

I started developing and printing my photos at the club, which was a lot of fun.

c _____
_____

Unfortunately, my parents didn't like the smell, so I stopped taking pictures for a while.

d _____
_____

The best thing is you can check your pictures instantly. Also, you don't have to buy film or pay for developing your pictures.

e _____
_____

It's a Canon digital SLR – it was very expensive, but it takes fantastic pictures!

3 Brainstorming

1 Before you start writing a text, it's a good idea to brainstorm ideas. You can do this by writing notes about your ideas. You can arrange your notes in different ways, e.g. lists. You can also use *idea maps*. Here is an idea map for the topic in exercise 1:

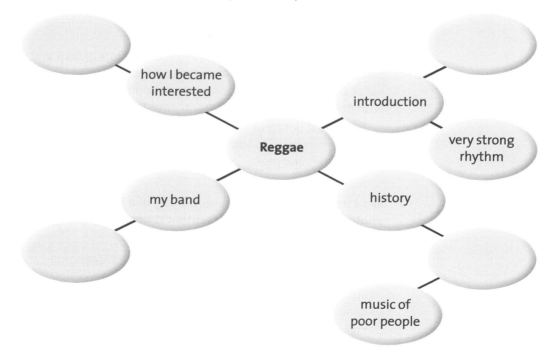

how I became interested

introduction

Reggae

very strong rhythm

my band

history

music of poor people

2 *Reggae* is the main topic of the text. It is connected to four sub-topics. Write the details of the sub-topics in the correct bubbles:

started in the 1960s
a type of popular music
guitarist, play original songs and covers
parents' old records

3 Work with a partner. Complete the idea map below with these notes:

two types (stiff and flexible)
go to the park twice a week
types of skateboard
other equipment
started in the 1960s in California
history
skateboarding and me
helmet, knee and elbow pads

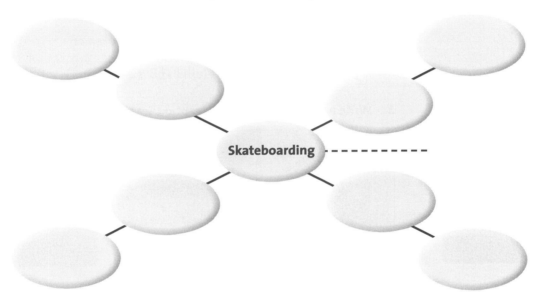

4 Add bubbles for the ideas below in the idea map above.

skateboarding tricks
popular with surfers
wood / fiberglass / plastic
kick-flips

5 Work with a partner. Use the idea map to write a text about skateboarding for an Internet home page.

4 Writing about photographs

1 You can write a caption for a photograph like this:

This is me and my new camera.

This was taken at my 18th birthday party.

Dave is on his skateboard.

This is a picture of my favorite skateboard.

2 Or shorten it like this:

Me and my new camera.   (omit *This is*)
My 18th birthday party.   (omit *This was taken at*)
Dave on his skateboard.   (omit *is'*)
My favorite skateboard.   (omit *This is a picture of*)

3 Write a short version of each caption for each photograph below.

1 This is my brother Jack and our dog.

_____

2 This was taken on my graduation day.

_____

3 Mom and Dad are playing tennis.

_____

4 This is a picture of my first car.

_____

4 Now add a suitable second sentence to each caption.

Don't we look happy!
Isn't she a beauty?
Jack is the one on the right.
Wimbledon finals!

5 Writing task

 1 Choose one of the topics below or think of your own topic, and make an idea map. Write about a personal interest for a personal home page.

2 Find two or three photographs to illustrate your text. If you can't find photographs, draw simple sketches. Write captions for the photographs.

15 Applying for a job

1 A job application from a student

1 Read the advertisement and application letter.

VP   VICTOR PUBLICATIONS

Graphic designer

Victor Publications seeks a talented graphic designer to join its Hong Kong design team. Excellent opportunity for a college graduate. Applicants should speak English and at least one Asian language. Excellent salary and benefits.

Apply with résumé to:
Jessica Wong
Personnel Manager
Victor Publications
Garden House
202 Kings Road
Quarry Bay
Hong Kong

Dear Ms. Wong,

I would like to apply for the position of graphic designer advertised in the November 23 issue of the *Asian Times*. I enclose a copy of my résumé, as requested.

As you can see from my résumé, I will graduate from art university next February. Although my work experience is limited, I believe I have the necessary skills for the position of Assistant Designer. I speak English, Japanese, and Korean.

I look forward to hearing from you.

Sincerely,

Miho Taguchi
Miho Taguchi

2 **Answer the questions.**
  a What job is advertised?
  b How many Asian languages should the applicant speak?
  c What should he / she send?
  d Where did Miho see the advertisement?
  e Which Asian languages does she speak?

2 Changing jobs

1 Read the advertisement.

ELT Times September 10 | 2004

WESTMINSTER

UNIVERSITY PRESS

Sales Representative

The English Language Teaching Sales Department of Westminster University Press is looking for an experienced person to work as a sales representative in Mexico City. Applicants should be fluent speakers of English and Spanish, and have an interest in language learning and teaching.

Apply with résumé to: Jésus Fernández, General Manager, ELT Sales Department

2 Fill in the blanks in the application letter, using the words below.

requested   see   enjoyed   like
worked   work   learned   enclose

Dear Mr. Fernández,

I would like to apply for the position of Sales Representative advertised in the September 10 issue of the *ELT Times*. I ^a_____ a copy of my résumé, as ^b_____ .

As you can ^c_____ from my résumé, I have ^d_____ for Pathfinder Publications for two years.

Although I have ^e_____ my time there as a sales representative, and have ^f_____ a great deal about the publishing business, I would now like to look for new challenges. I would also ^g_____ more chances to improve my English skills.

I would very much like to ^h_____ for your company, and I hope that you will consider my application.

I look forward to hearing from you.

3 The shaded words or phrases in the letter have the same or a similar meaning to the ones below. Write the matching items on the correct lines below.

a industry _____
b extend my skills _____
c opportunities _____
d think about _____

e am writing to _____
f a lot _____
g CV _____
h post _____

4 Rewrite the letter, using the phrases from exercise 3.

NAOMI TAGAWA

3-1 Nagayama 2-chome
Tama-shi, Tokyo 206
Tel: +81(456)78-9012
Email: ntagawa@nifty.co.jp

EMPLOYMENT OBJECTIVE

Full-time position as bilingual secretary

EDUCATION

2001– present	Owada University, Tokyo Bachelor of Arts (Expected February 2005) Major: English Literature
1998 – 2001	Ichikawa High School, Chiba

EMPLOYMENT EXPERIENCE

2001 – present	Digital Soft Inc. Tokyo (part-time) Administrative Assistant Duties include English business correspondence, translation, and some clerical work
1999 – 2000	Sweaters Sports Club, Tokyo Receptionist Duties included dealing with telephone inquiries, processing membership applications, and supervising equipment rental

SKILLS

Working knowledge of Microsoft Word and Excel.
English: TOEIC score 720, STEP (Eiken) 1.5

INTERESTS

Tennis, reading, photography

REFERENCES

Available on request

2 Are these statements true (T) or false (F)? Check (✓) the correct box.

		T	F
a	Naomi wrote her address at the top of the page.	☐	☐
b	She wrote the title of the job she was applying for.	☐	☐
c	She wrote about her education after her work experience.	☐	☐
d	She described the type of work she did in each job.	☐	☐
e	She wrote about her hobbies.	☐	☐
f	She enclosed references with her résumé.	☐	☐

4 Ellipsis

LANGUAGE FOCUS

Since the résumé is only about you, you can omit the pronoun *I*, auxiliary verbs (*am, was*), and the possessive *my*. You can also often omit articles (*a, an, the*):

I worked as a part-time cashier. ▸ *Worked as part-time cashier.*

Write these sentences in the same way.

a   I can operate both PCs and Macs.

_____

b   I was promoted to senior clerk.

_____

c   My duties included clerical work.

_____

d   I was appointed office manager in June 2004.

_____

e   I wrote movie reviews for the student magazine.

_____

f   I am studying mechanical engineering.

_____

5 Vocabulary

1 The words and phrases on the right are often used in résumés. Match each one with a word or phrase with a similar meaning on the left.

a	be familiar with	1	operate	☐
b	use	2	assist	☐
c	have responsibility for	3	have a working knowledge of	☐
d	help	4	handle	☐

2 Rewrite these sentences using the words and phrases in the right-hand column in the previous exercise. Omit words such as *I*, if necessary.

a   I *helped* the office staff with computer maintenance.

_____

b   I *had responsibility for* customer inquiries.

_____

c   I *used* a PC for word processing and spreadsheets.

_____

d   I *am familiar with* Microsoft Word and Excel.

_____

6 Writing task 1

Choose one of the four jobs and write an application letter. Use your own ideas.

Galaxy Hotels ★★★

Reception staff

Organization: Galaxy Hotels

Location: Rome, Berlin, Singapore

We are looking for people who enjoy working with others, and can communicate in English and at least one Asian language. Successful applicants will be based in one of the locations above, and duties will include dealing with guests' inquiries and organizing hotel events. Training is provided.

APEX Computers

Designer

Organization: Apex Computers

Location: California

We need a creative and enthusiastic person to join our award-winning design team. Experience in product design is not essential. The successful applicant will work on designs for a variety of products.

MUSIC MAKER

Music correspondents

Organization: Music Maker magazine

Location: London, Sydney, Tokyo, Seoul

Each correspondent will be based in one of the cities above and interview visiting bands and musicians. Applicants must be able to write in English and have a wide knowledge of contemporary popular music.

WORLD AID

Aid worker

Organization: World Aid

Location: Tanzania

We are seeking a young person to work in Tanzania for two years as an assistant primary school teacher. The successful applicant will work at a number of schools and assist local teachers. Applicants should be hard-working and independent. Teaching qualifications are not essential, and training will be provided.

7 Writing task 2 Write your own résumé.

Review 3

1 Describing a place

1 Read the email quickly. Which of these statements is true?
Check (✓) the correct box.

a Mi-Sun is living in a big apartment. ☐
b All her classmates are Korean and Japanese. ☐
c She has joined some university clubs. ☐

To: Dave Nosworthy <nosworthyd@hotmail.com>

Cc:

Subject: Hello from Stanford University!

Arial   10   B I U ⊞ ▾ | ⋮≡ ⋮≡ ⋮≡ | ≡ ≡ ≡

Dear Dave,

Well, I started the theater studies course ᵃ_____ week.
There are thirty other students taking the course – from all over
the world.

The ᵇ_____ campus is really big. It has a hospital and a
shopping ᶜ_____ !

I'm ᵈ_____ in a small apartment in Palo Alto. The
neighborhood is busy, and there's ᵉ_____ to do in the
evenings.

My classmates are ᶠ_____, and I've joined a few clubs and
ᵍ_____ .

I'll only be here for one ʰ_____ , but I'm sure I'm going to
learn a lot!

Write ⁱ_____ ,

Mi-Sun

---

2 Complete the email with these words.

university	semester	plenty
societies	staying	great
center	soon	last

2 Recommendations

1 **Read the email quickly. Answer the questions.**

a Does Dave use the reply function?

b Which places does he recommend?

c What can Mi-Sun do at Lake Lagunita?

2 **There is one mistake (punctuation, capitalization, spelling, grammar, or a missing word) in each sentence below. Circle it, then rewrite the complete correct sentence. When you have finished, talk to a partner and compare your work.**

a The university, snowboarding society is a lot of fun.

_____

b Have you hear about the new Thai restaurant?

_____

c The new Radiohead CD is excellent – I highly recomend it.

_____

d The food were cold, and the service was awful.

_____

e I liked the comfortable seats and the big screen?

_____

f The *Paper Moon* bookstore has a good selection of books and a great café, to.

_____

3 Pairwork dictation

1 Work with a partner. Take turns reading sentences to your partner, who will write them down. Student A, use the sentences on the page 105. Student B, use the sentences on page 106.

> **USEFUL LANGUAGE**
>
> Could you say that again?
> Could you speak more slowly?
> How do you spell "…"?
> What's the (fourth) word?

Write your partner's sentences here:

a _____

b _____

c _____

d _____

e _____

f _____

2 When you are finished, compare your sentences with your partner's page. Did you write everything correctly?

4 Word puzzle

Write the answers to the clues below in the puzzle. When you are finished, read down to find the answer to this question:

What do you write to describe a photograph or illustration?

a My apartment is very near the university c_____ .

b Jack is so h_____-working . He studies for hours every day.

c I sent my résumé to Microsoft's p_____ manager.

d While I was w_____ for the plane, I met my English teacher.

e Before you write, it's a good idea to b_____ for ideas.

f The t_____ sentence is usually the first sentence of a paragraph.

g I hope that you will c_____ my application.

5 A thank-you email

1 Are these statements true (T) or false (F)? Check (✓) the correct box.

		T	F
a	Noriko is writing to her friend.	☐	☐
b	She is making an inquiry.	☐	☐
c	She enjoyed writing a home page.	☐	☐
d	She uses a formal salutation.	☐	☐

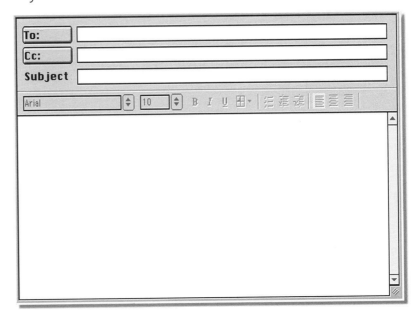

To: padulac@yahoo.co.jp
Cc:
Subject: Thank you

Arial | 10 | B I U ⊞▾ | ☷ ☷ ☷ | ☰ ☰ ☰

Dear Ms. Padula,

Thank you very much for the course. I really enjoyed it and I learned a lot. I think my spelling and punctuation have improved!

One of the most interesting things in the course was learning how to write a personal home page.

Best wishes,

Noriko Abe

2 Write a similar email to your teacher. Thank him / her and mention:
— one or two things about your English writing that have improved (spelling, punctuation, grammar, writing style)
— one of the most interesting things in the course (learning how to write …)
— your own ideas.

To:
Cc:
Subject

Arial | 10 | B I U ⊞▾ | ☷ ☷ ☷ | ☰ ☰ ☰

6 Writing and culture: the Internet

1 In Unit 14, you practiced writing for your personal home page. These people are writing about other ways to write on the Internet.

I sometimes write to news websites about the latest news. I like seeing my email on the web page. My favorite website is the BBC *Have your say* page – people write in from all over the world.

I'm a New York Yankees fan, and I joined the fans' message board a couple of months ago. I like writing a short message, then getting replies right away from other fans. I often spend hours online!

I live in Boston and my sister lives in Los Angeles, so we spend a lot on phone bills. We occasionally use "instant messaging" to save money. We talk online for about an hour. It's fun, but I prefer speaking on the phone.

I want to start my own blog soon. *Blog* is short for *weblog*, and most blogs are diaries for everyone to read. It's very easy to input new information. My brother's blog is really interesting. Yesterday he wrote about his breakfast(!).

2 Talk to a partner.

Do you …
— write to news websites?
— belong to a message board?
— use instant messaging?
— keep a blog?

If the answer is *no*, ask:
Do you want to …

3 Write a short paragraph about the type of Internet writing you do, or want to do in the future.

Pairwork dictation

Student A

Review 1

Student A, read these sentences to your partner:

a   I would like to tell you about my family.
b   In the future, I want to write letters in English.
c   I look forward to meeting you next week.
d   Thanks for helping me.
e   I hope to hear from you soon.
f   Could you send me a copy of your catalog?

Review 2

Student A, read these sentences to your partner:

a   I'm looking forward to seeing you in September.
b   Thank you for the invitation.
c   Please fax the information to (541) 346-1092.
d   I am writing to complain about my order.
e   Go three stops on the Chuo line.
f   I hope you will give me a refund.

Review 3

Student A, read these sentences to your partner:

a   I'm staying with a really nice family.
b   This CD is fantastic – check it out!
c   In Rome, we visited some famous places and ate great pizza.
d   Reggae is popular all over the world.
e   I enclose a copy of my résumé as requested.
f   This is me and my family at my graduation!

Pairwork dictation

Student B

Review 1

Student B, read these sentences to your partner:

a   Thanks in advance for your help.
b   I am hoping to stay in San Francisco for three days.
c   I saw your advertisement in the December 12 *New Scientist*.
d   I am a Business Studies student at Waseda University.
e   Please send me a copy of your prospectus.
f   I like playing baseball and going to the movies.

Review 2

Student B, read these sentences to your partner:

a   I have a few questions about the weather.
b   I'm afraid I'm busy Saturday.
c   I would like to apologize for any inconvenience.
d   I am still waiting to receive my books.
e   Get off at the last stop.
f   You'll see a department store on the left.

Review 3

Student B, read these sentences to your partner:

a   My apartment is near the station, which is convenient.
b   The new bakery store downtown is worth a visit.
c   The beaches in Thailand were crowded, but beautiful.
d   I started to play the guitar a few years ago.
e   I have a working knowledge of English and German.
f   I look forward to hearing from you.

Reference section

Section 1 Formats

Emails

---

1 Writing an email

When you write an email your computer will look something like this:

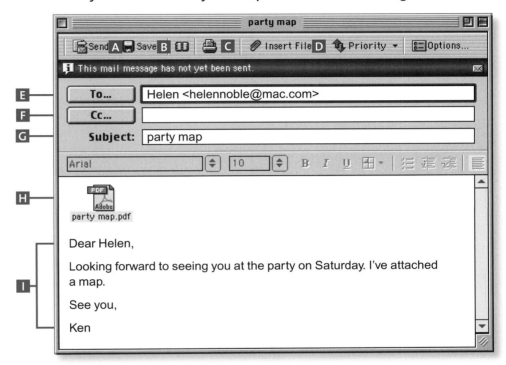

Click this when you want to …

a   send your message.
b   save your message.
c   print your message.
d   attach a document (text file, photographs, etc.)

This is where you …

e   write the name of the person you are writing to.
f   write the names of other people who will receive the same message.
g   write what the message is about.
h   see the title of a document (text file, photo, etc.) which is sent with the email message.
i   write the body (main text) of the message.

2 Receiving an email

When you receive an email, your computer screen will look something like this:

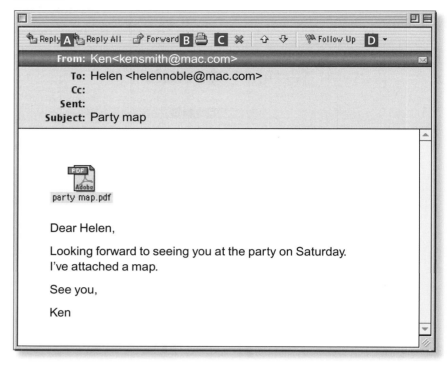

Click this when you want to ...

a reply to the message.
b send the same message to another person.
c print a copy of the message.
d remember an important message.

3 Using the reply function

When you click the "reply" button, the body of your email might look like this:

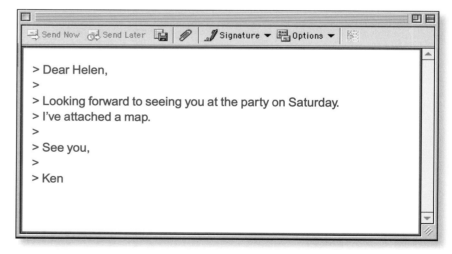

You can edit (change) the message you received when you reply to someone. For example, Helen uses the main body of the email, but changes the salutation, complimentary close, and signature:

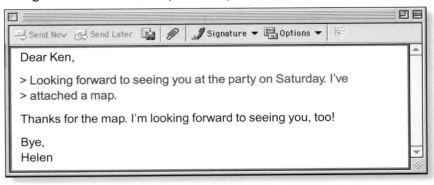

Letters

1 Writing a personal letter

You can use the same layout for letters written by hand or on a computer:

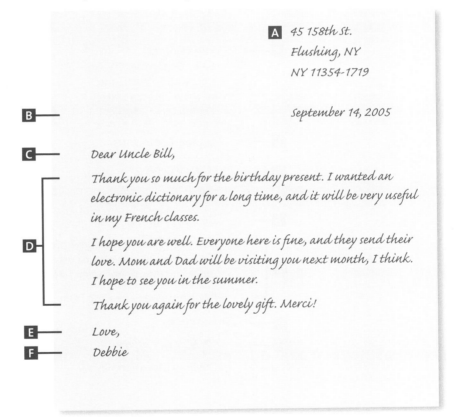

a Heading: Your address. This is not necessary if you use letterhead writing paper.
b Date: Write this on the right, under your address. Leave a space between your address and the date.
c Salutation: Capitalize the first word and the name, and use a comma at the end.

* Indent = leave five blank spaces at the beginning of a line (one tab on a word processor)

d   Body: Start a new paragraph for each topic. You can indent* the first line of each paragraph if you like.
e   Closing: Position this on the left-hand side of the page. Start with a capital letter, and write a comma at the end.
f   Signature: Your own name. Even if you write a personal letter on a computer, sign it by hand.

2 Writing a business letter

A business letter should be written on a computer.

If you do not know the name of the person you are writing to, use *Dear Sir or Madam*. End with *Sincerely*, and sign yourself with your full name. If you know the person's name, use *Dear Mr. / Ms.:* , and end with your full name.

The simplest business letter format is the full-block format. In this format all the parts of the letter (except for your own address) are lined up on the left-hand side of the paper:

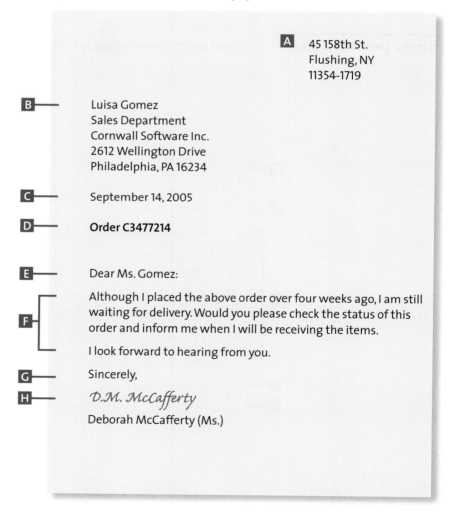

A 45 158th St.
Flushing, NY
11354-1719

B Luisa Gomez
Sales Department
Cornwall Software Inc.
2612 Wellington Drive
Philadelphia, PA 16234

C September 14, 2005

D **Order C3477214**

E Dear Ms. Gomez:

F Although I placed the above order over four weeks ago, I am still waiting for delivery. Would you please check the status of this order and inform me when I will be receiving the items.

I look forward to hearing from you.

G Sincerely,

H *D.M. McCafferty*
Deborah McCafferty (Ms.)

a   Heading: Your address. This is not necessary if you use letterhead paper.
b   Inside address: The full name and address of the person you are writing to.

c	Date:	Write this on the left, under the address of the person you are writing to. Leave a gap between their address and the date.
d	Subject line:	This is optional (you don't have to use it).
e	Salutation:	Use the person's title (Mr., Ms., Dr., etc.) and a colon or comma at the end. A colon is more formal.
f	Body:	Start a new paragraph for each topic. You can indent the first line of each paragraph if you like.
g	Closing:	Position this on the left-hand side of the page. Start with a capital letter, and write a comma at the end.
h	Signature:	Write this by hand. Type your full name below your handwritten signature.

3 The envelope

You can use the same layout for personal and business letter envelopes:

*Some other special instructions:

CONFIDENTIAL
REGISTERED MAIL
SPECIAL DELIVERY
PRINTED MATTER

a Sender's full name and address. Write this clearly.
b Postage stamp(s).
c Full name and address of the person you are sending the letter to. Write this clearly. You can write all of this section in capital letters if you like.
d Special instructions.*

Fax cover sheets

You can write an informal fax cover sheet by hand:

October 21, 2006

Victor,

I saw this article in the paper yesterday — thought you'd be interested!

See you soon,
Sandra

When you send a fax to a company or organization, include a heading with your message. You can save your heading as a template:

1-26-54 Jinan
Shibuya-ku
Tokyo 150-8571
Japan

Tel/fax: +81 3 4462 7100
e-mail: ssaltz@gol.com

To	Elizabeth Pei
From	Stephanie Saltz
Subject	catalog
Date	February 5, 2005
No. of pages	4

Dear Elizabeth,

I found the office equipment catalog you asked about, and I'm sending you copies of the pages about printers.

Let me know if you can't read them.

Best wishes,

Stephanie

Postcards

The reverse side of a picture postcard usually looks like this:

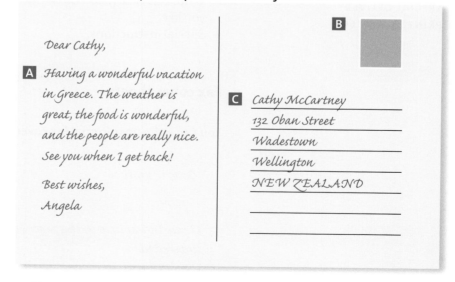

Dear Cathy,

Having a wonderful vacation in Greece. The weather is great, the food is wonderful, and the people are really nice. See you when I get back!

Best wishes,
Angela

Cathy McCartney
132 Oban Street
Wadestown
Wellington
NEW ZEALAND

a Message.
b Stamp(s).
c Address.

People often send postcards when they go on vacation. Messages are usually:

— short: three or four sentences
— informal, e.g. use of incomplete sentences
  Having a great time in … / Wish you were here
— descriptive, e.g. use of adjectives.
  wonderful, hot, relaxing, boring

Here are some typical messages …

to family:

> *Dear All,*
>
> *Marco and I are having a great time here in Tahiti. We've been relaxing on the beach, but I've been scuba-diving and water-skiing, too. It's beautiful here, and I wish I could stay longer. See you soon.*
>
> *Love,*
> *Maria*

to a teacher:

> *Dear Ms. Marques,*
>
> *I'm having a great time in Vancouver. I'm really enjoying the English classes, and my host family is very kind. I think my English has improved a bit! I hope to see you again next semester.*
>
> *Best wishes,*
> *Natsuko (Terada)*

to colleagues:

> *Hi everyone!*
>
> *Here we are in Paris. Went to Disneyland yesterday. Tomorrow we're going to see the Mona Lisa in the Louvre. We're taking lots of photos!*
>
> *All the best,*
> *Dave*

to a close friend:

> *Pete,*
>
> *How are you? Wish you were here. Ibiza is amazing! We're going clubbing every night! I'd like to stay all summer.*
>
> *See you,*
> *Andy*

Internet home pages

Here is a site map for a personal Internet home page:

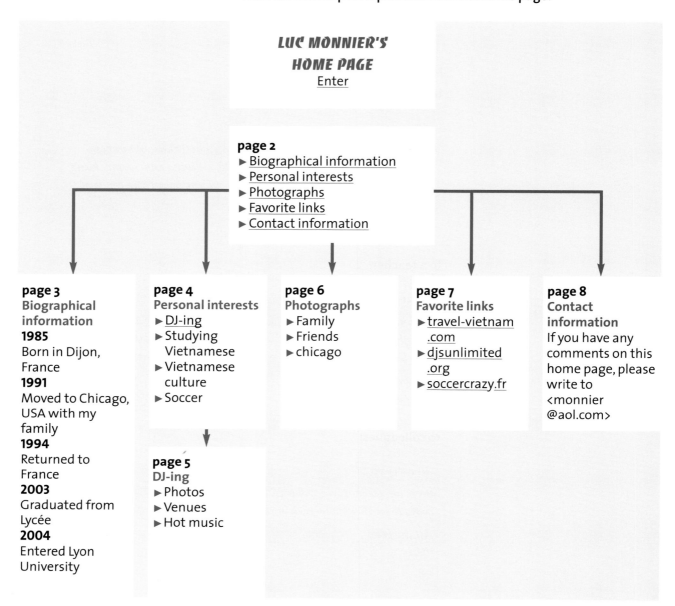

LUC MONNIER'S HOME PAGE
Enter

page 2
► Biographical information
► Personal interests
► Photographs
► Favorite links
► Contact information

page 3
Biographical information
1985
Born in Dijon, France
1991
Moved to Chicago, USA with my family
1994
Returned to France
2003
Graduated from Lycée
2004
Entered Lyon University

page 4
Personal interests
► DJ-ing
► Studying Vietnamese
► Vietnamese culture
► Soccer

page 5
DJ-ing
► Photos
► Venues
► Hot music

page 6
Photographs
► Family
► Friends
► chicago

page 7
Favorite links
► travel-vietnam.com
► djsunlimited.org
► soccercrazy.fr

page 8
Contact information
If you have any comments on this home page, please write to <monnier@aol.com>

Some important points to remember when you make your home page:
Make sure:
— you keep it simple – don't use too many fonts, colors, or background patterns
— it is easy to read and easy to use
— all the graphics and links are working correctly
— you update the site regularly
— you think carefully about the personal information you put on your home page. Remember anyone can read it.

School compositions

The standard American style for writing a school composition or report by hand looks like this:

A

B *Marco Spinetti*
C *English 101*
D *Professor Gretsky*
E *May 5, 2004*

F *My Favorite City: Venice*

Venice is a beautiful city. It has around 200,000

G *visitors every day. It was built on marshland, and*

there are a lot of canals.

There are no cars in Venice. The best way to

travel is by boat – by gondola (very romantic!) or by

vaporetto. However, it is also very nice to walk.

a   Left margin. This is usually red. Don't write to the left of this line. The teacher can use this space for comments.
b   Your name. Write your first (given) name, then your last name.
c   The name of the class.
d   The name of the teacher.
e   The date.
f   The title of your composition.
g   The main body of your composition:
   — indent the first line of each paragraph
   — double space your lines (your teacher can make comments and corrections)
   — leave some space at the end of each line.

Job résumés

Before you send off a job résumé, ask yourself these questions:
— Is it well-organized?
— Is it easy to read?
— Are there any spelling mistakes?

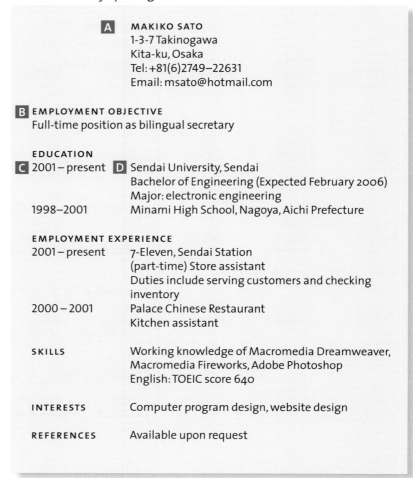

A   MAKIKO SATO
1-3-7 Takinogawa
Kita-ku, Osaka
Tel: +81(6)2749–22631
Email: msato@hotmail.com

B EMPLOYMENT OBJECTIVE
Full-time position as bilingual secretary

EDUCATION
C 2001 – present   **D** Sendai University, Sendai
Bachelor of Engineering (Expected February 2006)
Major: electronic engineering
1998–2001   Minami High School, Nagoya, Aichi Prefecture

EMPLOYMENT EXPERIENCE
2001 – present   7-Eleven, Sendai Station
(part-time) Store assistant
Duties include serving customers and checking
inventory
2000 – 2001   Palace Chinese Restaurant
Kitchen assistant

SKILLS   Working knowledge of Macromedia Dreamweaver,
Macromedia Fireworks, Adobe Photoshop
English: TOEIC score 640

INTERESTS   Computer program design, website design

REFERENCES   Available upon request

a   Write your full name, street address, telephone number(s), and email address.
b   Write headings in capital letters, and start at the left margin.
c   Write dates on the left margin. Put the most recent date at the top of each section.
d   Set the information in each section one or two centimeters to the right, to allow space for dates.

The résumé is only about you, so you can shorten sentences like this:

I attended French classes.	— *Attended French classes.*
My duties include …	— *Duties include …*
I was responsible for …	— *Responsible for …*
I have a working knowledge of Adobe Photoshop.	— *Working knowledge of Adobe Photoshop.*
I was awarded the Gold Prize.	— *Awarded Gold Prize.*

Section 2 Common features of written English

1 Salutations and closings

1 Business letter or email

SALUTATION

If you know the person's name:

Dear + title + family name + colon or comma	Dear Mr. Vronsky: Dear Ms. Berg: Dear Mr. Vronsky, Dear Ms. Berg,

If you don't know the person's name:

Dear + Sir or Madam Dear + person's position Dear + department name Dear + company name	Dear Sir or Madam: Dear Personnel Manager: Dear Personnel Department: Dear Amazon:

CLOSING

Sincerely, Sincerely yours,	+ your handwritten signature (full name) + your typewritten name	Sincerely, *Jessica Wong* Jessica Wong

2 Formal social letter

SALUTATION

Dear + title + family name,	Dear Ms. Everett, Dear Prof. Evans, Dear Dr. Berg,

CLOSING

Sincerely, Sincerely yours,	+ your handwritten signature (full name):	Sincerely, *Jessica Wong*

3 Informal letter

SALUTATION

Dear + given name,	Dear Setsuko,

CLOSING

Best wishes, Kind regards,	+ your signature (given name):	Best wishes, *Yuri* Kind regards, *Hideo*

4   Informal email

SALUTATION	
Dear + given name, Given name,	Dear Brad, Brad, Hi! (very informal)

Note: If you often write emails to someone you know well, you can omit a salutation.

CLOSING		
See you, Bye for now,	+ your given name:	See you, Linda Bye for now, Pedro

---

2 Beginnings and endings

1   Business letter or email

BEGINNING
(new subject) I am writing about … (reply) I am writing in response to your letter of January 22, 2005. Thank you for your email dated October 5, 2005.

ENDING
Thank you once again. I look forward to hearing from you.

2   Formal social letter or email

BEGINNING
(new subject) I am writing about (next week's lecture). (reply) Thank you for your email dated March 10, 2004. I was very pleased to hear from you.

ENDING
I hope to meet you again in the near future. I look forward to hearing from you. Please give my regards to everyone.

3 Informal social letter or email

BEGINNING

(new subject)
How are you?
Hope you are keeping well.*
(reply)
Thanks for your email.
Good to hear from you.

*In informal writing, we can leave out the subject *I* in *I hope* …

ENDING

See you soon.
Write soon!
Take care.
Regards to everyone!

Section 3 | Capital letters, punctuation, and spelling

1 Capital letters

Use capital letters (upper case):

— at the beginning of a sentence:
This is a pen.

— for names of people, schools, and companies:
Fidel Castro; Chancellor's School; Harrods

— for brand names and products:
Starbucks; Panasonic; Kit-Kat

— for a person's title:
Mrs. Ghandi; Dr. Winterbotham; Prof. Ozaki

— for some abbreviations:
CEO (Chief Executive Officer), M.A. (Master of Arts)

— for names of countries, places, and streets:
Paraguay; Central Park; Elm Street

— for the main words in titles of movies, books, songs, and magazines:
Jaws; War and Peace; The Harder they Come; Time

— for days of the week, months of the year, and special days:
Tuesday; August; Labor Day

Use only capital letters (block capitals) when you fill out forms by hand:

JOHN SMITH
14 ST BERNARD'S ROAD
BIRMINGHAM B92 7BB
UK

2 Punctuation

Punctuation makes your writing easier to understand. The most common punctuation marks are:

1 Period (.)
Use a period:
— at the end of a complete sentence, when this is a statement:
I'm leaving for Europe tomorrow.

— after an abbreviation:
Mr. Ms. Dr. Prof. etc.

— in units of money:
$5.99   €35.50

— in units of time (UK):
8.30   10.00

— in email and website addresses:
sjprice@hotmail.com   www.oup.com

2 Comma (,)
A comma shows a short break in a complete sentence. Use it in a long sentence before a linking word like *but* or *so*:
I wanted to buy some milk, but the store was closed.
I was very tired, so I went straight to bed.

You can also use it in a list:
I want to visit France, Italy, and Germany.

Use a comma after the salutation in an informal letter or email:
Dear Ms. Perez,   Dear Andy,

Use a comma after the complimentary close in any letter or email:
Sincerely,   Sincerely yours,   Best wishes,   Bye for now,

3 Question mark (?)
Use a question mark at the end of a *yes/no* question, or a *wh*-question.
Are you busy Sunday?
What are you doing Sunday?

4 Exclamation mark (!)
Use an exclamation mark at the end of a sentence to show surprise, shock, or pleasure:
Eminem was sitting at the next table!
The car crashed right in front of us!

5 Colon (:)
Use a colon before a list or quotation:
The campus has good sports facilities: a swimming pool, a gymnasium, and tennis courts.
He shouted: "Don't be late!"

And after the salutation in a formal business letter or email:
Dear Mr. Parkinson: Dear Sir or Madam:

6 Semicolon (;)
Use a semicolon to connect two clauses when the second clause gives extra information about the first:
I felt terrible after the flight; I had a headache and my legs hurt.
Hee-Yun is really good at English; she always gets top marks.

7 Apostrophe (')

In informal writing, use an apostrophe to show contractions:
That's a great idea.

Use an apostrophe to show possession:
Have you seen Pim's laptop?
The dog's nose was cold and wet.

If the word or name ends with an *s*, you can show possession in two ways:
Is that James' house?   Is that James's house?

8 Quotation marks (" ")

Use quotation marks before and after direct speech (the exact words someone says). Quotation marks contain the words and the punctuation (period, question mark, exclamation mark, etc.):
"It's on the table."
"Where's the police station?"

Do not use quotation marks in reported speech:
He said it was on the table.
She asked us to be quiet.

9 Parentheses ( )

Use parentheses to add extra information to a sentence. Notice that the sentence is still complete without the information in parentheses:
I met Jeff the other day (he was here on vacation).
I want to visit some art galleries (especially Tate Modern), and go to the theater.

10 Dash (–)

In informal writing, you can use a dash in the same way as parentheses. If the additional information comes at the end of the sentence, use only one dash:
I met Jeff the other day – he was here on vacation.
I want to visit some art galleries – especially Tate Modern – and go to the theater.

11 Hyphen (-)

A hyphen joins words in a compound word and numbers in a compound number: (a hyphen is shorter than a dash).

mother-in-law   medium-sized
thirty-five   seventy-one

---

3 Spelling

If you write on a computer, you probably use a spellchecker. If you don't have an English spellchecker, here is some useful advice on spelling.

1 Common spelling mistakes

People often spell these words incorrectly:

accommodation	*definitely*	*embarrassed*	*grammar*
misspell	*noticeable*	*receive*	*sandwiches*
separate			

People often use these possessive forms wrongly:
Incorrect: *The house has it's own pool.*
Correct: *The house has its own pool.*

Incorrect: *They came in they're new car.*
Correct: *They came in their new car.*

Incorrect: *Is that you're dictionary?*
Correct: *Is that your dictionary?*

2 Adjectives with final *l* and adverbs with *ll*
Always use one *l* at the end of an adjective:
hopeful   awful   careful

But use a double *l* in the adverb form:
hopefully   awfully   carefully

3 *ie* and *ei*
When *ie* and *ei* have a long *ee* sound, you can use this rule:
i before e, except after c.
believe   chief   field   niece   piece

But when *ei* sounds like *ay*:
neighbor   weigh

After *c*, write *ei*:
ceiling   receive   receipt

4 Plurals: words ending in *y*
If there is a vowel (*a, e, i, o, u*) before the *y*, add an *s* to make the plural:
boy – boys   day – days   key – keys

If there is a consonant (*b, c, d,* etc.) before the *y*, change the *y* to *i* and add *es.*
baby – babies   country – countries   memory – memories

5 Verb forms: Simple present
Don't forget to add *s* to the 3rd person singular (*he / she / it*) form:
eat – eats   read – reads   leave – leaves

With verbs ending in y, change the *y* to *ies*:
carry – carries   try – tries   fly – flies

There are some irregular verbs:
do – does   go – goes

6 Verb forms: *ing*
With most verbs, add *ing*:
eat – eating   read – reading   study – studying

With most verbs ending in *e*, drop the *e*:
have – having   hope – hoping   leave – leaving

With verbs ending in one *l*, just add *ing*:
feel – feeling   travel – traveling   sail – sailing

With verbs ending in *ie*, change *ie* to *y*:
die – dying   lie – lying

7 Verb forms: Simple past tense
With most regular verbs, add *ed*:
walk – walked   reach – reached   return – returned

With regular verbs ending in *e*, add *d* only:
save – saved   live – lived   phone – phoned

You must learn irregular verbs individually:
drive – drove   go – went   shine – shone

8 Compound nouns

Sometimes when we use two words together, the two words may become one word:

goodbye   *businessman*
email   *wordprocessing*

Section 4   **Functions**

1 Expressing likes and dislikes (Unit 1)

I   really like … .
    like … .

I think …   is OK.

I   don't like … very much.
    don't like … .
    hate … .

2 Thanking (Unit 4)

FORMAL

I am writing to thank you	for	helping me with my presentation.
		the wonderful dinner.
Thank you very much		the beautiful birthday present.

INFORMAL

Thanks a lot	for	helping me with my presentation.
Thanks		the fantastic dinner.
		the beautiful birthday present!

3 Requesting (Unit 5)

FORMAL

Could	you please send me	more information about your school?
Would		
Please send me		a complete list of language courses.

INFORMAL

| Could you | send me another copy of the picture? |
| | let me know your new street address? |

4 Recommending 1 (Unit 6)

FORMAL

I recommend   a taxi.
            you take a taxi.

INFORMAL

You can Make sure you	eat at try	the local restaurant. the seafood.
Bring Don't forget	warm clothes. your sun hat!	

5 Inviting (Unit 7)

FORMAL

Would you like	to go to a party Saturday evening? to join us for a meal tomorrow evening?

INFORMAL

Would you like Do you want	to go	swimming on Monday? out for a pizza tonight?
How about	going	

6 Accepting and refusing an invitation (Unit 7)

1 Accepting

FORMAL

Thank you very much for the dinner invitation.
I would be delighted to accept.

INFORMAL

Thanks for inviting me. I'd love to have dinner.

Dinner sounds	great! like fun!

2 Refusing

FORMAL

Thank you very much for the dinner invitation, but I am afraid I am unable to come.

INFORMAL

Thanks for inviting me, but I'm afraid I'm sorry but	I can't make it.

7 Apologizing for changing plans (Unit 8)

FORMAL

I am very sorry, but I am afraid I am unable to attend the meeting tomorrow.

INFORMAL

I hate to say I can't join you for the movie tomorrow night.

I'm sorry, I can't make it.

8 Complaining and requesting action (Unit 10)

1 Complaining

I am writing	to complain about about a problem with	the service in your Boston restaurant.
	with reference to about	a printer I bought in your store two days ago.

2 Requesting action

Would you please	send a replacement give me a refund	as soon as possible.

I hope you will agree to replace the sweater free of charge.

9 Recommending 2 (Unit 12)

The movie The exhibition The new store	is excellent. is very good.	I highly recommend it. I recommend it. Check it out.
	is average.	OK, but nothing special.
	isn't very good.	I don't recommend it. Give it a miss.
	is terrible.	I don't recommend it at all.

Section 5 General

1 Days, dates, and times

1 Days
Always use a capital letter at the beginning of a weekday:
Monday, Tuesday, Wednesday, etc.

In a list, you can use the first three letters (+ period) :
Mon.   Arrive in Tokyo
Tue.   Visit Kamakura
Wed.   To Osaka

In a regular sentence, use the full word:
Are you doing anything on Saturday?
Looking forward to seeing you on Friday.

2   Months

Always use a capital letter at the beginning of a month:
August, September, October, etc.

In a list, you can use the short form (three letters + period):

Apr. 9	*First semester begins*
Jul. 12	*First semester ends*
Sep. 8	*Second semester begins*

3   Years

In a regular sentence you can use the full written form, but this is very unusual:
I think we first met in nineteen eighty-nine.

In most writing, the full numeral form is more common:
1998, 2001, 2008

You can use the short form (apostrophe + final two numerals) in informal messages:
See you in '06!

4   Dates

At the beginning of a letter and in a regular sentence, write the date like this:
November 14, 2005
We got married on April 26, 1999.

Use the numerical form* only on forms or for informal letters or emails:
11/14/05
4/26/99

5   Times

In a regular sentence, you can write the hours like this:

Let's meet at	*six o'clock.*
	6 o'clock.
	6 p.m.
	6 o'clock p.m.

And the quarter and half hour times like this:

How about	*a quarter past six?*
	half past six?
	a quarter to seven?

But most writers use numerals only with a colon. You can add a.m. or p.m. if you like:

How about	*6:00? / 6:00 p.m.?*
The train leaves at	*9:23 / 9:23 a.m.*

***Important**
In American English, the order is always month / day / year. In British English, the order is always day / month / year.

6 Prepositions

on + day:	*Where should we meet on Friday?*
on + date:	*We are leaving on July 24.*

Note: In American English you can omit *on* in informal writing:

Where should we meet Friday?
We're leaving July 24.

in + month:	*I was in Australia in August.*
in + year:	*She graduated in 2002.*
at + time:	*See you at 7 o'clock.*

2 Numbers

In formal writing, spell out numbers from 1 through 100:
Felipe is twenty-one next month.
There are fifty states in the United States.

Use numerals for larger numbers:
My grandfather is 110 years old.
The dictionary has 1,992 pages.

In lists and informal writing, you can use numerals for all numbers.

Note the positions of the commas in these numbers:
219 (no comma)
111,219
141,219
141,219
3,141,219

3 Prices

In formal writing, write out smaller prices (under 100 dollars):
Membership is ten dollars.
We paid fifty dollars for the tickets.

Use numerals for larger prices, and place the dollar sign before the number:
My new computer cost $1,249.
Last month I earned $900!

Use numerals and a period for prices which include cents:
It cost $5.25.
The list price was $99.99.

In lists and informal writing, you can use numerals for all prices.

4 Currencies

COUNTRY	CURRENCY	SYMBOL
Australia	Australian dollar	$
Brazil	real	R$
Canada	Canadian dollar	$
EC (European Community)	euro	€
Hong Kong	HK dollar	$
Indonesia	rupiah	Rp
Japan	yen	¥
Korea	won	W
New Zealand	NZ dollar	$
Thailand	baht	Bht / Bt
United Kingdom	pound	£
United States	U.S. dollar	$

5 Abbreviations

1 Length

cm.	centimeter(s)
m.	meter(s)
km.	kilometer(s)
in.	inch(es)
ft.	foot, feet
mi.	mile(s)

2 Time

a.m.	ante meridiem (before noon)	11 a.m.
p.m.	post meridiem (after noon)	6:30 p.m.
min., mins.	minute, minutes	
hr., hrs.	hour, hours	

3 Points of the compass

N., S., E., W.	north, south, east, west
NE., SW., etc.	northeast, southwest, etc.

4 Common abbreviations from Latin

e.g.	*exempli gratia* (for example)
etc.	*et cetera* (and more in the same way)
i.e.	*id est* (that is, in other words)
NB	*nota bene* (note well, take notice)
vs.	*versus* (against)

5 Personal titles

B.A.	Bachelor of Arts	*David Wang, B.A.*
B.S.	Bachelor of Science	*Veronica McTavish, B.S.*
M.A.	Master of Arts	*Keiko Takayama, M.A.*
Mr.	Mister	*Mr. William Davis*
Mrs.	Married woman	*Mrs. Deborah Davis*
Ms.	Woman (married or single)	*Ms. Rosetta Garcia*
Ph.D.	Doctor of Philosophy	*John Smith Ph.D.*

6   Others

fwd.	forward
cc.	copy
re:	about, concerning
p., pp.	page, pages
No., no.	number

7   Some common symbols

#	number	*Ref. #3652*
@	at	*bcrumb@gol.com*
*	asterisk – to mark a note	*Price: $250 **
		(*batteries not included)
"	inch, inches	*6" × 4" photos*
'	foot, feet (twelve inches)	*The table is 5' long and 3' wide.*

8   Text-messaging

ABBREVIATION	DEFINITION	ABBREVIATION	DEFINITION
ATB	All the best	JK	Just kidding
ATM	At the moment	KIT	Keep in touch
B4	Before	L8	Late
B4N	Bye for now	L8R	Later
BBL	Be back later	NP	No problem
BTW	By the way	O4U	Only for you
BF	Boyfriend	PLS	Please
C	See	R	Are
CU	See you	RU	Are you
CUL8R	See you later	SPK	Speak
DK	Don't know	SPK2 U L8R	Speak to you later
DUR	Do you remember?	THX	Thanks
EVRY1	Everyone	U	You
EZY	Easy	UOK	are you OK?
F2T	Free to talk	U2	You too
GR8	Great!	WOT	What
GF	Girlfriend	WTG	Way to go!
H8	Hate	WUF	Where are you from?
H&K	Hugs and kisses		
IC	I see	W8	Wait
IDK	I don't know	X	Kiss
ILU	I love you	Y	Why?
ILU2	I love you too	YR	Your
J4F	Just for fun	ZZZZZ	Sleeping

6 American English and British English differences

The most important differences are in spelling and vocabulary:

1 Spelling

The main differences in spelling are:

	AMERICAN ENGLISH	BRITISH ENGLISH
-or / *-our*	color, neighbor, favorite	colour, neighbour, favourite
-z- / *-s-*	organization, recognize	organisation, recognise
-er / *-re*	theater, meter	theatre, metre
-l- / *-ll-*	canceled, labeled, traveler	cancelled, labelled, traveller

2 Vocabulary

Some useful examples:

AMERICAN ENGLISH	BRITISH ENGLISH
apartment	flat
cellphone	mobile phone
(potato) chips	(potato) crisps
cookie	biscuit
drugstore	chemist
elevator	lift
first floor	ground floor
French fries	chips
gasoline, gas	petrol
one-way ticket	single (ticket)
parking lot	car park
period (in punctuation)	full stop
sidewalk	pavement
subway (train)	underground, tube

3 Writing a business letter

	AMERICAN ENGLISH	BRITISH ENGLISH
Salutation	Dear Mr. Baker, OR (formal business letter) Dear Mr. Baker:	Dear Mr Baker (no period after Mr) (no comma after the name)
Closing	Sincerely, OR Sincerely yours,	Yours faithfully OR Yours sincerely (no comma)

7 Country and city names

In English, some country and city names are spelled (and pronounced) differently to the original language. Here are some examples:

COUNTRY NAME		CITY	
(original)	(English)	(original)	(English)
Belgique	Belgium	Antwerpen	Antwerp
Deutschland	Germany	München	Munich
		Köln	Cologne
Hellas	Greece	Athinai	Athens
Italia	Italy	Venezia	Venice
		Firenze	Florence
Österreich	Austria	Wien	Vienna
Polska	Poland	Warsawa	Warsaw
Suisse/Schweiz/Svizzera	Switzerland	Genève	Geneva

8 International street addresses

Here is a U.S. address:

Ms. Veronica Chung
12 Forest Court
Mill Valley, CA 94941
USA

The name of the state is usually written as two letters:

CA	California	CO	Colorado	CT	Connecticut
FL	Florida	MA	Maryland	TX	Texas

Here are some addresses in other countries:

South Korea:
Mr. Kim Sung-Sook
Pacific Engineering Ltd.
Room 126 Sunshine Building
1–85 Nonhyon-dong
Kangnam-ku
SEOUL 150-320
KOREA

United Kingdom:
Mr. S. J. Hamnet
Star Publishing Ltd.
22 Bristow Gardens
LONDON W8 8PD
U.K.

Japan:
Mr. Jiro Endo
Edomizaka Mori Bdlg 6F
4-1-40 Toranomon
Minatu-ku
Tokyo 105-8529

Australia:
Stavros and Melina Kariotakis
16 Soudan St.
Bardon
Queensland
AUSTRALIA 4065

9 Internet addresses (URLs)

An Internet address or URL (Uniform Resource Locator) usually looks like this:

http://www.apple.com
http://www.bbc.co.uk
http://www.elt@oupjapan.co.jp

When we write an Internet address in an email or letter, we often use pointed brackets like this: <http://www.apple.com>. The last part of the address is called the *domain*, and can tell us something about the website.

Some important U.S. domains are:

.com*	Commercial (companies and for-profit websites)
.org*	Non-profit organizations
.net*	Network access groups (e.g. Internet service providers)
.gov	Federal governmental agencies
.edu	Educational institutions granting 4-year degrees (often .ac in other countries)
.mil	Military agencies and organizations

*These three domains can now be used by anybody!

There are also 2-digit country domains. If there is no country code, the organization is probably based in the United States. Some examples of country domains are:

.uk	United Kingdom
.kr	Korea
.jp	Japan
.au	Australia
.ca	Canada
.nz	New Zealand
.cn	China
.de	Germany
.fr	France

Notes

Write down key words and expressions that you want to use and remember.

1 Thinking about writing

_____
_____
_____
_____
_____
_____
_____

2 Introducing

_____
_____
_____
_____
_____
_____
_____

3 Completing forms

_____
_____
_____
_____
_____
_____
_____

4 Thanking

_____
_____
_____
_____
_____
_____
_____

5 Requesting information

_____
_____
_____
_____
_____
_____
_____

6 Getting details

_____

_____

_____

_____

_____

_____

_____

7 Inviting and arranging to meet

_____

_____

_____

_____

_____

_____

_____

8 Making and changing arrangements

_____

_____

_____

_____

_____

_____

_____

9 Giving directions

_____

_____

_____

_____

_____

_____

_____

10 Dealing with problems

_____

_____

_____

_____

_____

_____

_____

11 Describing

_____
_____
_____
_____
_____
_____
_____

12 Giving an opinion and recommending

_____
_____
_____
_____
_____
_____
_____
_____

13 Writing about a vacation

_____
_____
_____
_____
_____
_____
_____
_____

14 Writing about an interest

_____
_____
_____
_____
_____
_____
_____
_____

15 Applying for a job

_____
_____
_____
_____
_____
_____
_____

OXFORD
UNIVERSITY PRESS

Great Clarendon Street, Oxford OX2 6DP

Oxford University Press is a department of the University of Oxford.
It furthers the University's objective of excellence in research, scholarship,
and education by publishing worldwide in

Oxford New York

Auckland Cape Town Dar es Salaam Hong Kong Karachi
Kuala Lumpur Madrid Melbourne Mexico City Nairobi
New Delhi Shanghai Taipei Toronto

With offices in

Argentina Austria Brazil Chile Czech Republic France Greece
Guatemala Hungary Italy Japan South Korea Poland Portugal
Singapore Switzerland Thailand Turkey Ukraine Vietnam

OXFORD and OXFORD ENGLISH are registered trade marks of
Oxford University Press in the UK and in certain other countries

© Oxford University Press 2004

The moral rights of the author have been asserted

Database right Oxford University Press (maker)

First published 2004
2008 2007 2006 2005 2004
10 9 8 7 6 5 4 3 2 1

ISBN 0 19 453814 1

Printed in China

ACKNOWLEDGEMENTS

*The authors and publisher are grateful for permission to reproduce the following
extracts and adaptations of copyright material:* p18 Hotmail Registration
Form. Screen shot reprinted by permission from Microsoft
Corporation; p33 UK Landing Card. Crown copyright reproduced with
the permission of the Home Office.

Sources: pp16-17 I-94 US Immigration Form from
http://uscis.gov/graphics/formsfee/forms/index.htm

*The publisher would like to thank the following for their permission to reproduce
photographs and other copyright material:* Alamy Images pp4 (man with
laptop/David Yound-Wolff), 58 (red London bus/Photofusion Picture
Library); Arena PAL p31 (Love's Labours Lost/John Timbers); Corbis
pp41 (Husky Stadium/P J Corwin), 9 (man with guitar/Lucidio Studios
Inc.), 96 (woman in turtleneck/Elizabeth Young), 88 (man with guitar);
Getty Images pp87 (New Zealand lake/Taxi), 75 (teacher in
class/Photodisc); John Birdsall Social Issues Photo Library p38 (family);
OUP pp8 (man snowboarding/PhotoDisc), 9 (girl smiling/Photodisc),
9 (boy cycling/Digital Vision), 14 (Dallas/PhotoDisc), 15 (Hawaii/
PhotoDisc), 16 (filling out form/PhotoDisc), 41 (Capitol building/
PhotoDisc), 41 (White House/PhotoDisc), 49 (Grand Canyon/Corel),
51 (airplane landing/PhotoDisc), 52 (Montreal/Société de Transport de
Montreal), 55 (London underground map/London Transport Museum),
89 (dog/PhotoDisc), 92 (young friends photographed/Digital Stock),
92 (skateboarding/PhotoDisc), 92 (skateboard/PhotoDisc), 92 (people in
nightclub/PhotoDisc), 92 (man with dog/PhotoDisc), 92 (friends
graduating/ PhotoDisc), 92 (tennis game/PhotoDisc), 92 (small car/
PhotoDisc), 96 (girl smiling/PhotoDisc), 96 (man smiling/Photodisc),
96 (girl smiling/Digital Vision), 96 (girl smiling/PhotoDisc), 49 (country
porch/PhotoDisc), 104 (teenage boy/Image Source); Retna Pictures Ltd
pp88 (Bob Marley), 88 (Aswad).

Cover photography by: OUP (students on campus/PhotoDisc), (girl in
wetsuit/PhotoDisc), (girl in front of a computer/Imageshop); Pierre
d'Alancaisez (keyboard & letter); Punchstock (man with laptop using
mobile phone/Komstock).

Illustrations by: Mark Duffin: pp23, 56, 56, 57, 59, 67, 69, 77, 78, 80;
Roger Penwill: pp5, 13, 17, 21, 24, 25, 29, 38, 43, 44, 45, 52, 61, 63, 65,
71, 83, 85, 86, 87, 93, 99